Feeling Good Again

A Workbook For Children Who Have Been Sexually Abused

By Burt Wasserman

SaferSocietyPress

PO BOX 340
BRANDON, VERMONT 05733-0340

Design & Typesetting: Sue Storey Design & Illustration
Editor: Euan Bear
Printing: United Book Press, Inc., Baltimore Maryland

ISBN: 1-884444-51-2
$16.00
Bulk discounts available.

Order from:
The Safer Society Press
P.O. Box 340
Brandon, VT 05733
802-247-3132

Also available: *Feeling Good Again Guide for Parents and Therapists*
ISBN: 1-884444-52-0
$8.00

Acknowledgments

Many wonderful clinicians have reviewed this workbook and provided feedback about what they do with the children they work with. As they did, this workbook grew. I would like to thank Philip Davidson, Joan Duhaime, Joanne Glass, and Ruth Varner for their feedback and contributions.

Special thanks also go to Yvonne Dolan and Lucia Capacchione who both have wonderful books on healing for survivors of sexual abuse, and who graciously gave permission for their work to be adapted or reprinted in this workbook.

A very special thanks to Gail Ryan, Director of the Perpetration Prevention Project at the Kempe National Center. As a leader in the treatment of sexually abusive youth, her feedback, guidance, and editing are greatly appreciated.

My special gratitude goes out to Judith Smith, Ph.D., who took this workbook on her vacation to review and provided some additional editing changes. As well as being an excellent presenter, Judith was a co-investigator on a three year NIMH research project examining the impact of sexual abuse on girls ages six through twelve. She is currently the director of a hospital-based behavioral health program in northwest Pennsylvania.

I would also like to express my gratitude to all the program administrators at hospitals and Community Service Boards who supplied their staff with this workbook. Your confidence enabled me to stay with it and let it grow.

Publisher's Thanks

As always, we are indebted to our wise and experienced colleagues for their review and feedback. In particular, we offer our thanks to Gail Ryan in Colorado, Carolyn Cunningham in California, and Lynn Sanford in Masachusetts for their careful reading and insightful comments. Without the generous contribution of time and expertise of these colleagues and many others, it would be much harder to carry out our mission of making available the best in treatment and training publications, teaching offenders to control their harmful behaviors, helping victims to feel good again, and making society safer for all of us.

About The Safer Society Press

The Safer Society Press is part of The Safer Foundation, Inc, a 501(c)3 private, nonprofit national agency dedicated to the prevention and treatment of sexual abuse. Founded in 1964 by Quaker activist Fay Honey Knopp, the Safer Society Press has continually tracked emerging issues and underserved populations in the field of sex offender and victim treatment. The Safer Society Press publishes an extensive collection of treatment-oriented books, audiocassettes, and videotapes for clinician training and victim and offender treatment. For a catalog, write to The Safer Society Press, PO Box 340, Brandon, VT 05733, call 802-247-3132, or visit our Website at www.safersociety.org.

Contents

SECTION ONE

SECTION TWO
Part I: Dealing with Your Feelings

Part II: From Victim to Survivor

Part III: Feeling Good Again

Part IV: More Questions

Summary

We Begin
Learning Together

feeling powerful

This book is for you. It is a book that may help you feel more powerful.

Powerful feelings come from talking, drawing, being in the playroom, and learning about your feelings.

Can you remember a time when you felt really POWERFUL?

You always want to be able to remember those powerful feelings, and keep them close to you.

Some children find that when they make pictures of the times that they felt powerful in the past and keep those pictures close to them, it helps them be strong enough to talk about the thing that happened to them.

What were the times that you felt powerful? Draw a picture of one of those times you had a powerful feeling.

You may want to start each session with your counselor by looking at your picture and bringing the powerful feelings into your body.

Picture developed

some thoughts about good touching

We can never get enough of good touching.

It makes the world go around and it makes life beautiful. Good touching helps us to feel lovable and teaches us how to love others.

Good touching makes us feel good.

Good touching goes with warmth, love, caring and safety.

Whatever has happened to you in the past, you may want to remember that there can also be good touching in your life … in the future.

Good touching may not be something you know much about.

You may know more about bad touching, which is what this book is about.

It is important to understand what bad touching is so that you can recognize it and get people to do something about stopping it.

The more you know about bad touching, the more you will be able to give and receive good touching.

Good Touching is Love.

a difficult time

Something bad happened to you. It is sad that some girls and boys go through what you did.

Understanding what happened to you will take time. It is my wish that this workbook will help you learn what happened, so you can go on with your life and be safe.

Your counselor has chosen to use this workbook as a guide to help you understand things better.

This is not a book that you should read quickly. The real learning will happen when you and your counselor take time and talk about each chapter.

There may also be other things that you need to know that are not in this book.

Your counselor will know what these things are, but you also need to tell your counselor what you need to know.

If you don't understand something in this book, it's **ALWAYS** okay to ask your counselor or one of your parents for help.

So take your time reading this book and pat yourself on the back for all you are about to learn.

the problem

Being sexually abused can be like a nightmare that really happened! Like nightmares, the more you talk about them, the less of a problem they become.

The first thing you need to know about your problem is that working with a counselor can help.

The counselor you are working with has been trained to help children who are experiencing bad feelings. These counselors have a special name: they are called therapists. A therapist is someone who has been trained to help people feel better.

Section One
Chapter 1

You Are Not Alone

This workbook has been written for you and your counselor. It will help you with the feelings that many children experience after they have been sexually assaulted.

When children have been sexually abused they may not like to talk about what happened. When they remember the abuse they may feel bad all over again.

One nice thing about working with someone specially trained is they've already heard experiences like yours from other children.

You can tell your therapist anything and your therapist will help you understand it better.

Remember, your therapist has probably heard an experience like yours before.

Most children who have been sexually abused are surprised to learn that what has happened to them has happened to many other children.

It is important for you to know ...

You are not alone!

Sometimes children who have been abused still feel alone even though they know the same thing happened to other children.

They feel alone because they feel that they have no friends. Some children didn't have the chance to make friends because their family was busy keeping secrets and staying private. Other children don't feel okay talking to their friends anymore because of what they have been through.

Making friends will take time. As you feel better able to deal with what happened to you, you may find it is becoming easier to make friends.

Chapter 2

Talking About It

Children may not like to talk about nightmares because they may be afraid they will happen again. Talking about abuse sometimes feels like that.

The more you talk about what happened, the more you will understand it. As you begin to talk about the abuse, the picture in your head may be very big and scary. Talking about it may make your picture smaller, more blurry and not so scary. It becomes a memory of the past, not something bad happening right now.

Talking about what happened can get the uncomfortable feelings out of your body so you can stop walking around with them.

But talking about it can also be very difficult.

Don't be surprised if things come out ... a little at a time. Don't rush yourself. Take all the time you need.

When children first tell their about being abused they often talk about it happening only one time. Sometimes that's because it only did happen once.

Sometimes that's because telling about one time is all they feel they can talk about at first. They want to see what their counselor does before they tell more.

Children sometimes feel too afraid to tell about everything that happened. As you develop a trust for your counselor you will be able to tell your counselor more about what happened to you during the abuse. You may feel good that you can tell the whole thing out loud.

Sometimes it is so difficult to talk about what happened, it is easier to draw what happened.

Some therapists have dolls in their office so you can show them what happened without so many words.

Which do you think would be the easiest way to tell your therapist what happened?

_____✓____Talk _____ Draw _____ Show with dolls

What kind of uncomfortable feelings do you have when you think about what happened to you?

Feelings:

1._____   4._____

2._____   5._____

3._____   6._____

Talking about the abuse may also help keep you safe.

Sometimes children don't talk about the abuse. They may not want to hurt other people's feelings or make someone angry.

Children who have been abused or neglected may have been taught by their parents to put other people's feelings first.

They may be taught that their own feelings are not important.

It's a good thing that you may not want to hurt other people's feelings.

But.... **Your Feelings Are Important Too.**

You shouldn't have to suffer to protect another person's feelings.

Some of the people whose feelings you want to protect, like one of your parents, might be happy to know that you trust them enough to share that you are hurting.

Sometimes children don't talk about what happened to them because they are ashamed. They think it was their fault.

Even though lots of people have told you it's not your fault, you need to remember **why** it's not your fault.

Do you know why it was not your fault?

Some children **still** think it was their fault because they liked the person who abused them.

They also might have liked some of the touching.

Some children who were sexually abused didn't know this kind of touching was wrong and the person who was doing it was wrong.

It seemed okay when it was happening.

They got angry when they realized the person they trusted was doing something wrong.

Some girls feel guilty because they think or someone told them they acted "sexy" or dressed that way, and they think that's why the abuser picked them.

Other children think they should have yelled or screamed. They feel guilty they didn't.

Some children feel they should have been braver and fought harder.

Sometimes children feel even worse when their abuser was the same sex.

Or they think they should have enjoyed being abused when their abuser was the opposite sex.

Whatever your reason was for any kind of guilty feeling, you need to remember one thing:

IT WAS NOT YOUR FAULT!

You are brave because you have already told somebody about the thing that happened to you.

By telling someone you can help keep yourself safe.

You might even help keep this from happening to someone else and you can feel good about that.

In order to feel better it is important to understand what you are feeling and why you might be confused and angry.

Children who have been abused often have some awful experiences to tell.

Some children are even afraid to tell their therapist. They are afraid their therapist won't like them anymore.

Please don't be afraid to tell about your whole experience.

Your therapist will understand and won't stop liking you.

Sometimes when feelings come out it feels better at first but worse later on. You might feel like taking the words back. The mixed up feeling you may get will go away because your counselor will help you learn how to handle the feelings that came out.

The next chapters talk about what kind of things might happen after children have been sexually abused and what you can do to deal with them if they happen to you.

Chapter 3

Dealing With Your Feelings

One of the first things that can happen to children who have been sexually abused is they get confused about their feelings.

Some children aren't sure what they feel.

Do you know what feelings you have about the abuse?

Listed below are some of the feelings that sometimes go with sexual abuse.

Have you had any of these feelings?

Anger   Shame

Sadness   Numbness

Confusion   Powerless

Embarrassment   Betrayal

Fear   Guilt

Anxious   Worry

Vulnerable   Unsafe

Sometimes children who have been abused think they deserved what happened to them. Sometimes they even think they are worthless or no good.

Sometimes they think that because the person who abused them told them those things.

If you start to have those awful thoughts, put them in a cloud, and let them float away, or put those feelings back in the past where they belong, with the abuser.

What negative thoughts about yourself have you had in the past?

Are you ready to put them in a cloud so they can float away?

Or do you want to give them back to the person they belong to: the person who abused you? Yes

What helpful, encouraging and caring words can you say to yourself instead of the negative words?

I am
nice
friendly
Popular
Pretty
active
lots of friends
Pretty eyes
Helpfull
encouraging

When children talk about what happened, it helps to get those feelings out of their bodies so they don't have to walk around with them all the time.

Most children have mixed feelings when they talk about the abuse. That means having more than one feeling at the same time.

Although it feels good once the feelings are out, at the same time, it can still hurt to talk about what happened.

These mixed feelings are confusing for children who often don't want to talk about what happened to them in every session.

anger

Some children were not angry when the abuse happened. But they started to get angry when they found out how the abuser tricked or betrayed them.

Sometimes the amount of anger also changes when you talk about the abuse.

Some children get more angry than before, and then after awhile that anger begins to go away.

If 10 marbles represent the most anger you could have about anything. How many marbles worth of anger did you have at these times? Color them in.

At the time the abuse happened ...

When you found out it was wrong ...

After you talked to someone about it ...

After you told the person who did it how angry you are . . . .

How many marbles worth of anger do you have today about the abuse?

You may want to remember some of the angry feelings and that is ok. You can hold on to them as long as you feel you need to.

How much of the angry feelings do you think belong in the present?

all because of if I hear his name I blow up

Are there memories about the abuse that will help you be safer? *yes*

What memories of the abuse will help you to be safer?

the anger makes me stronger

all because of the anger

Feeling uncomfortable or scared may be a signal that there is something wrong and that it could help to do something about it ... like talk to someone.

Talking to someone helps get the feelings out. Then you can figure out what made you feel unsafe.

Remember, don't be discouraged; it may take a long time to get all the feelings out that are hanging around from the past.

guilt

Some children felt special when they were with the abuser. The abuser told them they were special. Or the abuser did nice things for them, or treated them like grownups.

Children who were treated as special liked the person who ended up abusing them and had good feelings when they were with them. They may feel confused or guilty about those feelings.

It's natural to like someone who treats you special.

Maybe the abuser really did like you but didn't know the right way to let you know how he or she felt.

It's okay if the touching felt good to you — gentle touching usually does. You may not have known what the abuser was doing was wrong ... but he or she *did* know it was wrong. So the *abuser* is the one who should feel guilty, not you.

Other children feel guilty because of all the changes in their family once they told about the abuse. They think they caused it.

If you feel that way please remember that those feelings belong to the abuser, not to you. You don't have to carry them around any more.

43

shame

Shame is the feeling you have when you've done something you think is wrong. It gets worse when someone else finds out.

As someone who was abused, you didn't do anything wrong, the abuser did! So all that shame belongs to the abuser, not to you.

It is a good idea to get rid of every bit of any ashamed feelings. You didn't do anything wrong and it was not your fault.

Shame makes you feel worthless.

But you are worth a lot!

numbness

In the beginning, many children have no feelings about the abuse. They are "numb" to feelings about the abuse (numb means not feeling anything ... kind of blah, kind of gray and foggy).

It is like what the dentist does when he gives you a shot so you won't feel it when he has to fix a cavity and use the drill.

For some children, there were so many bad feelings connected to the abuse they needed to be numb and not feel anything.

For some children it was just too painful to think about, so they made themselves numb.

Other children are afraid what would happen if all their feelings come out at once.

Now that you are safe and not in any danger, you can let the numbness go away. You can take as much time as you want to let your feelings come out.

Instead of being afraid of being angry, think of anger as a mask. This angry mask covers up the feeling of not being safe.

When you can uncover those other feelings, you will find new and better ways to feel safe now, like ...

Draw a picture of a safe place.

Write a pretend letter to a safe person.

To:_____

From,

_____

Or . . . pretend the people who hurt you are in the room, and tell them how you really feel.

To:_____

inside time*

Listed below are some messages that might help you feel better. Which ones do you think you need to say to yourself so that you will remember and really believe it?

1. The sexual touching was not my fault.

2. I can feel better.

3. I am a good person.

4. It's not my job to protect grownups.

5. I am wiser and stronger than I was before the abuse.

6. My hurt feelings are fading away a little each day.

---

*This title and concept originated with Mindy Loiselle and Leslie Bailey Wright in *Shining Through: Pulling It Together After Sexual Abuse*. Brandon, VT: The Safer Society Press, 1995. Used by permission.

Some children say their message in front of a mirror ... until it sounds like they really believe it. Other children draw pictures to go with their message.

Some children draw the good feeling that comes into their body when they say their message. They use all the good feeling colors they can think of.

Ask your therapist for some big paper to draw your food feelings on.

Chapter 4

Feeling Crummy

Some children who have been sexually abused FEEL CRUMMY about their life and about themselves.

They might yell at their mothers, fight with their brothers, or have problems at school because they feel crummy and don't know what to do.

But guess what! What made them feel crummy was that the angry feelings they tried to make disappear were still coming out, only they didn't know it!

Trying to keep an angry feeling deep down inside your body is like trying to hold a beach ball under water ... It keeps coming up!

The crummy feelings you have had all this time may be the feelings about your abuse that never got a chance to get out.

One reason you may be working with a counselor is to try to prevent an abusive situation from happening again, and to allow those crummy feelings to go away.

If you have been feeling crummy for a long time, it may be hard for you to imagine how it would be to feel good inside ...

But, you might be curious about when that good feeling will start to fill your body.

There are some fun ways to make uncomfortable feelings go away. When you finish this book you will be ready to try some.

You might be curious to know just how easy it will be to make those feelings go away.

Some children feel so crummy they just want to end it all. These children may wish they were dead or try to hurt themselves with knives or pills or in other ways.

Did you ever feel that crummy?

Children who have those thoughts usually don't really want to kill themselves, they just want the pain to stop. They don't really want to be dead, they just want to feel better.

This workbook has been written to help you stop the pain or at least make it so you can deal with it.

If you still have those thoughts about hurting yourself or killing yourself, make sure you talk to your counselor right NOW!

You and your counselor may want to draw up a contract or an agreement that you can sign promising you will not hurt yourself and that you will call someone and talk to them if you are having those thoughts.

Chapter 5

Protecting Yourself

When children numb their feelings about the abuse, it's as if they were saying to themselves, "If it happens again, this way it won't hurt so much and I won't be able to feel anything."

But if they think it won't hurt anymore, they may not be as careful about protecting themslves.

But it may still hurt, deep down inside, and that hurt may have been coming out since you have been coming to counseling.

Always remember:

No one has the right to touch your private parts or any part of your body if that touching is making you feel uncomfortable!

You have the right to love and respect your body. You can be ANGRY at anybody who tries to make you change your mind about touching.

Your body is special. Nobody should be allowed to touch your body unless you want them to.

Older people should know this. It's their job to pay attention and not touch people without asking permission.

Now you also know.

There are many wonderful loving good touches that may also come your way.

You may want to talk to your counselor about good touches and bad touches.

Knowing that your body is special and that you can say NO! to someone, even if they are bigger and older than you . . . will make you STRONGER!

Another way of protecting yourself is to listen to your inner voice.

Your inner voice is made up of the thoughts and feelings you have deep inside your mind that tell you something is good or that it is wrong. When something is wrong, sometimes your inner voice feels like an icky feeling in your stomach, or a creepy feeling on your skin. When something is good and right, what does that feel like to you?

When something is wrong, tell someone.

You may have already found out that once you told someone who was ready to listen you could begin to feel safe.

To protect yourself in the future, you may need to turn up the volume of your inner voice so that once you feel something is wrong, you will keep telling people until *someone* listens.

If you don't think the person you tell believes you, keep talking to different people until someone does listen to you and believe you.

The important thing is to try your very best to watch out, look and listen for other children or adults who might hurt or abuse you. There is no guarantee you can always keep yourself safe all by yourself, but this will sure help.

For some children, the abuse happened for such a long time they thought that it would never end!

These children felt so sad and helpless that they wanted to die.

Did you ever feel that sad? Do these feelings still come back at times?

Counseling will help you know that you can be happy, you can feel lovable, just for yourself, and that you can feel safe.

It is the job of grown ups to keep all children safe from physical harm (not being hit or burned or put in danger). All children deserve to have people care about them and to trust people around them. Some adults, maybe even in their own families, cannot be trusted to do these things for the children who have been abused in their homes.

Sometimes, the only way to keep a child safe is for the child to move out of the home.

This really isn't fair. But it just may be the best way that grownups know to keep you safe.

your needs

One thing that helps prevent sexual abuse is when children and adults know what things need to happen for them to be safe.

What are your needs?

What do you need to happen in your life to feel safe?

Chapter 6

Why Me?

Children who were sexually abused may wonder ...
Why did this happen to ME?!

There is no good reason why this happened to you.

Sometimes bad things happen to good people for NO
REASON!

Some children think, "Maybe it was because I was too
pretty or handsome." So they decide they don't want
to be pretty or handsome anymore. They dress in
sloppy clothes or eat a lot or don't keep themselves
clean. Or sometimes they don't want to eat at all.
Other times they eat sweets to feel better.

The problem is that they weren't abused because of how they look. It was because the person who abused them was selfish and not caring about their feelings. That person needs help.

And changing the way you look won't keep an abuser from abusing you.

Both boys and girls need to know: Stuffing your feelings with food DOESN'T WORK! Not taking care of yourself doesn't help you be safe. It's okay to look good and to treat yourself well.

when boys are abused

When boys are abused by a bigger and older girl or by a woman, they might think they should have enjoyed it, because a GIRL did it.

These boys need to know that when those girls take advantage of being bigger and stronger, they are also being abusive.

Boys who are abused by an older girl have nothing to be ashamed of. It was abuse because the girl had more power.

When a bigger and older boy has abused them, they realize they were overpowered but they often wonder, "Why did he do that to *me?*"

These boys need to know there is nothing wrong with them. Being touched by another boy doesn't change who they are.

The simple fact is they were abused by another boy who was selfish and not caring about their feelings.

when girls are abused

Girls who were abused by another girl need to know that the girl was selfish and not caring about their feelings. There is nothing wrong with them. Being touched by another girl does not change who they are.

When girls are abused by boys or grown up men, those boys were also being selfish and not caring about their feelings.

Some children find it comforting that because they were brave enough to tell, they were able to make life safer for themselves and others. It doesn't always work out that way, but sometimes it really works.

Chapter 7

Why Did They Do It?

You have learned that the person who abused you is selfish and needs help. But how did that person get that way?

We don't really know why a person abuses a child. We do know that many abusers were abused when they were children. But not all of them were. And there are many, many people who were abused who never, ever abused anyone else.

The person who abused you may have been abused by someone else.

The difference between that person and you is ... that person probably didn't get counseling.

They didn't think anyone cared about their feelings, so they didn't care about your feelings.

That person's anger didn't come out in any counseling sessions (because the person didn't get any counseling). Instead it came out on YOU!

Because you told someone, that person may also get help, so other children won't be abused. So, now you know another reason for your counseling.

Remember, even though many abusers were victims as children, most children who were victims, like you, don't become abusers ... even when they don't get counseling.

Chapter 8

Touching Yourself

Another thing that often happens to children who are abused is that some children feel like they want to keep touching themselves on their private parts.

Usually this happens when they are still confused about the abuse.

All children are curious about their private parts. And touching yourself there is a natural way of learning about yourself.

Touching your private parts should not be about the abuse. If you cannot stop thinking about the abuse when you have those feelings in your private parts, tell your counselor! Your counselor can help you practice thinking caring thoughts about sexual behavior instead of abuse thoughts.

If you ever imagine that doing something sexual or hurting someone will make you feel better or will get back something you lost, tell someone. Tell someone like your counselor who can help you understand why those thoughts are not true and might even let you hurt yourself or someone else.

If it seems like you are touching yourself all the time ... or it feels like you can't stop when you want to ... or if you are touching yourself because you are angry or sad ... you need to talk about this with your counselor so the touching will stop being a problem for you.

It may also be helpful to tell your counselor what you were thinking about while you were touching yourself.

Sometimes when children are hurting, the thought they make up in their minds seem to hurt them even more.

If anything like this is happening to you, please ... let your counselor help you with this problem.

Chapter 9

Learning to Trust Again

The person who abused you may have been someone you liked and trusted. It hurts to know that person took advantage of you. You might really wish he or she didn't do it, or that you could forget it and be friends again, but that probably won't happen.

It may be very difficult to trust that person again. How does that feel to you?

It may not be okay to trust that person again ... but it will be okay to trust your own feelings again.

Your inner voice is now wiser and stronger so it will be easier to listen to your inner voice and trust it.

If you think your parent or some other grownup let you down, it's okay to be angry at them and it's okay to tell them you are angry.

It may take you a while to start trusting the person you think should have protected you.

But what about other people who never did anything to you. Should you trust them?

Or should you be cautious because you're afraid of getting hurt again?

Trusting other people will also take time … but remember … **most people are nice and are not out to hurt you.**

How do you decide who you can trust?

Chapter 10

Memories
That Hurt

With all the good work you have done to get those angry feelings out, you may still have some memories that hurt.

Bad memories can either hang around like a dark cloud …

Or they can jump back into your mind like a lightning bolt.

When they do, they are called "flashbacks."

Flashbacks can be helpful.

They give you information about what happened that you may have forgotten or blocked out.

The purpose of counseling has been to understand what happened in the past, to learn from it, and then to LEAVE IT IN THE PAST.

Since flashbacks bring the past back to the present, you need a way of dealing with them. One way to deal with flashbacks is to ask yourself these questions:

1. Why did this flashback come back now?

2. How is where I am now DIFFERENT from the time of the abuse?

3. Is there new information in this flashback that I need to remember?

4. What am I going to do now to feel better in the present?

When flashbacks come, uncomfortable feelings from the past come with them. What you always need to remember is …

You can do something about these flashbacks.

Even though flashbacks are painful … sometimes they are also helpful because they can give you more information about what really happened.

You will probably want to talk about the flashbacks with your counselor, but you may want to make them go away when you are alone.

Some children picture themselves putting the flashback in their pocket, so they can take it out later and talk about it with their therapist.

Once the flashbacks stop giving you new information it's okay to make them go away.

You don't have to keep feeling the same pain over and over again.

Making believe that something never happened or that it doesn't hurt any more when you think about it may have been important to help you get through the abuse.

But you don't have to keep on making yourself numb so you can't feel anything. When you are not numb you'll be able to have good feelings.

It is okay to teach yourself to bring a better feeling into your mind and body.

If bad feelings can come with bad memories ... then when you put a good memory into your mind, a good feeling will come with it.

The counseling sessions that you have had may have been painful and difficult but sometimes there were times that you really felt good about yourself.

Listed below are some good feelings that children often have as a result of counseling.

These good feelings can be used to help you remember good memories. You can use the good memories to deal with the flashbacks.

Courage	Pride
Self-confidence	Relief
Energy	Hope

The four ways you can bring good feelings back into your body are …

1. By using SELF-TALK to say nice things to yourself.

2. Remembering the good, helpful WORDS other people have said to you in the past.

3. Making PICTURES of good things in your head.

4. Remembering how your body experienced the good FEELINGS.

self-talk

What are some of the things you could say to yourself in order to bring a good feeling back into your body?

1. _____

_____

2. _____

_____

3. _____

_____

words

What words do you remember other people saying in the past that could help bring a good feeling back into your body?

1. _____

_____

2. _____

_____

3. _____

_____

pictures

What pictures could you put in your mind (to replace the pictures of the flashbacks), so that you can bring the good feeling back into your body?

Draw one of your good feeling pictures here.

Do you have another good feeling picture that you can draw on this page?

Another way you can bring a good feeling back is to go right to the part of your body where that good feeling starts.

For some children their good feeling starts near their heart, and for others around their head.

One child said he knows a good feeling is coming because of a tingling in his hands.

Sometimes just making a smile with your mouth will start a good feeling.

Teaching your body to remember a good feeling will get easier, the more you practice. Do you want to try it now?

The way that you do it, is to picture a time that you had a good feeling ... remembering your self-talk, the words other people were saying ...

And wait for the good feeling to show in your body.

Once that good feeling starts, stay with the feeling and enjoy it.

You can also play with the colors in the picture to see if the feeling gets even better when you change the colors.

You may even want to turn up the volume of your self-talk in your mind or the words you remember other people saying to make the feeling even better.

You may want to take your mind's eye and travel into your body to notice where that good feeling begins in your body.

When you have done everything in your power to make the good feeling even better, you can answer the questions on the next page about your feeling.

is it ...

Light	or	Heavy
Full	or	Empty
Warm	or	Cool
Smooth	or	Rough
Like an open flower	or	Like a closed flower
Fill your whole body	or	Fill part of your body

If your good feeling had a color, what color would it be?

Once you have taught your body to memorize a good feeling, you will be able to focus on the part of your body where that feeling starts, and bring it back into your body.

There is no "right way" or "best way" to bring the feeling back. The best way to do it is what works best for you.

While you may find that the best way is to go directly to your body to get the feeling back, other children find they have to bring the picture in their mind, first, before the feeling will come back.

Some children find the best way to get the feeling back is to remember their own self-talk or the words their counselor, parent, or loved ones have said in the past.

The children who use words try to find just a few to put in their self-talk. They find a few words they want to remember so they can pop little phrases into their minds.

What do you think will be the easiest way for you to bring the good feeling back?

Whenever you learn a new skill like bringing a good feeling back into your mind and body, it is important to practice it *before* you need to do it in an emergency. It's like practicing a fire drill at school *before* there's a fire, or practicing a song *before* you sing it to other people. It's like practicing your best basketball shot on the playground *before* you get in a game.

Then, when you really need it, you will be able to do it. If you practice this skill every night for a week, you will get better at it. You might even sleep better.

When you are practicing during the day, once you bring the good feeling into your body ... you can also imagine yourself in a situation where a flashback has occurred ... and watch yourself bring the good feeling back.

This skill will work in many other situations.

Whenever you are anxious, you can bring a calm feeling into your body to replace the anxious feeling.

Many children who have this skill use it at school, before they take a test or speak in front of the class.

Do you think you could use this skill at school?

Remember you can learn to be in charge of how you are feeling.

If a flashback comes, you can learn to take it away.

Chapter 11

From Now On

Sometimes children need to leave their home and live in a new home. A social worker or a judge has decided this is the only way they can be safe.

If you are one of those children, you need to know that there are many other children like you, who are living with new families and are learning they can be safe … and have a happy life.

What has happened to you in the past may have been very awful, but it is now … IN YOUR PAST!

You may never understand it, or forgive the abuser, or lose all your anger.

What happened to you was not fair.

But that is now in the past, and you have a new mission for the future.

Your mission is to leave all the uncomfortable feelings in the past and just take with you the learning that you need to keep.

Like other things that have happened to you in the past, when you get through a problem, you become stronger, wiser and better able to take care of yourself.

Other members of your family may have also learned some new things.

They may have learned that they need to always talk to you about what you are feeling.

They may have learned about good touching and bad touching and that some touching is not okay.

They may have learned that they also need to go to counseling.

If the abuse you experienced happened within your family, there are a lot of new rules for good touching that everyone in the family has to learn.

What are some new family rules that you and your counselor have discussed?

From now on, you can:

Feel good about yourself ...

Start to trust people ...

Be upfront about your feelings ...

And most important of all, remember what you have learned about keeping yourself safe and do the best you can to be with safe people and go to safe places.

Chapter 12

Feeling Good Again

There are many reasons for you to feel good about yourself. One reason is that you had the courage to get help.

Can you think of some other reasons? Write them here.

Some of the reasons you can feel good about yourself you might have learned in counseling.

Can you think of some? Write them here.

For some children, the abuse made them so sad, they forgot how to have fun.

What are some ways you will be having fun in the future?

Are there other people in your family or your neighborhood who will be safer because you had the courage to tell someone what happened to you?

I hope you **feel** like a hero because you **are** one for real.

Draw a picture of yourself having fun with other people that you have made safer.

Congratulations!

You have learned to love yourself and take care of yourself.

You have also helped to break the cycle of abuse.

You Did A Great Job!

Section 2:
Appendix

Brief Therapy
Interventions

Part 1

Dealing With Your Feelings

counseling & swimming*

Counseling is like swimming in a cold lake on a hot day. It's really tough to get started, and being in cold water (or in a counseling session) sometimes feels uncomfortable for a while ...

But as time goes by, the cold water doesn't feel so cold anymore.

How cold is the water in your counseling session today?

---

*Counseling & Swimming was written (with permission) as a result of attending a workshop presented by Esther Deblinger, PHD. This concept is mentioned in her book, co-authored by Ann Heflin, *Cognitive Behavioral Therapy for Sexually Abused Children* (Sage Publishing, 1996).

tears & laughter*

At times, talking to a counselor can be very difficult. Sometimes children cry during their counseling sessions.

Crying is good because it is a way your body has of letting some of the sadness out.

But counseling can also be fun and when the crying stops, that part of the session can be over and the next thing that you might do is … LAUGH!

---

*Tears & Laughter was written (with permission) as a result of attending a workshop presented by Esther Deblinger, PHD. This concept is mentioned in her book, co-authored by Ann Heflin, *Cognitive Behavioral Therapy for Sexually Abused Children* (Sage Publishing, 1996).

So whatever else happens, you can help your therapist make sure there is enough laughing in your counseling sessions.

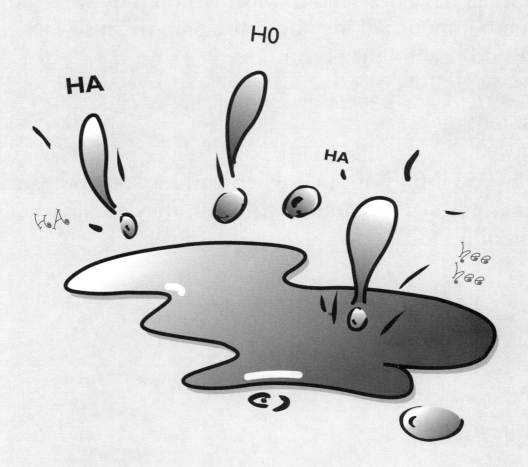

feeling the pain

When children's feelings are hurt, they try all sorts of ways to avoid feeling the pain. They make believe it didn't happen, or that it was a dream, or that it wasn't really so bad.

Some children even think that if it happened to them, they must have deserved it. Most children try to avoid remembering or talking about the pain because they are afraid it will hurt even more.

Maybe you'll find out that when you look at your hurt feelings and really stand up to them, they are less frightening.

Draw a picture of you standing up to those scary memories and feelings so they don't hurt anymore.

journal time*

Many children find that it really helps to write about the feelings they are having each day in their notebook or journal. Writing in a journal often helps because it gets the feelings out. For some children it's easier to start by writing about feelings than talking about them.

Once the feelings are out on the page, it may become easier to talk about the abuse.

*This title and concept originated with Mindy Loiselle and Leslie Bailey Wright in *Shining Through: Pulling It Together After Sexual Abuse*. Brandon, VT: The Safer Society Press, 1995. Used by permission.

getting your feelings out*

Sometimes children get so angry their feelings have a hard time coming out.

When they try to write their feelings, the real feelings don't come out.

Therapists who have helped many children dealing with sexual abuse have found a neat trick!

---

*Getting Your Feelings Out and Using the Other Hand concepts appear in *The Power of Your Other Hand* by Lucia Capacchione (Newcastle Publishing, 1988). Used by permission.

They found that when children write with their OTHER HAND their real feelings come out.

Those children said that when they write with their "other hand," a calm (everything will be all right) feeling comes into their bodies.

Since writing with the other hand is something most children don't do, it may be a good idea to start by writing your name.

using the other hand

The neat thing about writing with your other hand is that it is fun!

You know it will come out squiggly but that's okay.

Other people may not be able to read it but you will know what you wrote.

So get a magic marker or crayon and try doing these things with your other hand.

1. Write your name.

2. Write one feeling you have.

3. Write one thing you want to tell the person who abused you.

Can you think of anything else you want to write?

If you liked what came out on the paper you may want to do more things with your other hand.

Some children like to "Mirror Write" with their other hand. When you mirror write, the word you have written can only be read by holding the paper in front of a mirror. Try that in this box:

Other children like to draw pictures with their other hand:

Is there anything else you would like to do with your other hand?

Do you get a special feeling when you write with your other hand?

Some children who were sexually abused don't get help. When they get to be adults, they may have problems, like panic attacks.

One person I was working with started to have a panic attack (which is like a flashback) and she wasn't able to start writing with her other hand. Instead she *imagined* she was writing with her other hand and she told me IT WORKED!

If writing with your other hand was something that you found helpful ...

Imagining you are writing with your other hand may also help if you don't have any paper and pencils around.

sensations

Sometimes people know that good things are happening because of the sensations or feelings they have in their bodies. One person reported having a "tickling sensation" in his brain when he realized that "new things were happening." Another child felt a tingling sensation start in his hands when the good feeling started in his body.

Have you noticed any new sensations in your body when new ideas started to work for you?

drawing your feelings

Sometimes when children draw their feelings it gets their feelings out of their bodies and onto the paper.

Once you draw the angry feelings or the flashback feeling, you can start to think about what that feeling will change into when the angry and flashback feelings can't come back ... because the good feeling is already there instead!

What are the colors that go with your angry feeling?
Everybody's angry feeling looks different. What would
that angry feeling look like?

Are the colors of your flashback feeling different?
What does that look like?

What will your angry feeling look like when you turn it into understanding? What would it look like when you put a pleasant feeling in its place?

changing the picture

Sometimes if your flashback picture is about a person you are still afraid of, you might want to draw a picture of that person with a clown suit on ... and don't forget the funny makeup!

Keep changing the picture until the person is not scary anymore. Remember, the abuser is not scary any longer because the secret is out.

a bad apple

When children are abused, they may get very angry because they were "tricked." Some children get so angry that they take it out on other people.

If the abuser was a boy, they may not like or trust any boys and may think that other boys will also treat them in an abusive way. If the abuser was a man, they may be afraid to trust all men.

What is very sad is when the abuser represents a certain group like the Boy Scouts or their church. Some children develop a fear, or a distrust for the whole group, rather than keeping those feelings just for the abuser.

If you are in this situation, you might want to think of the abuser as a bad apple in a bushel basket full of nice, sweet, shiny, healthy apples. If you take away the bad apple, the rest of the apples will be fine.

If the abuser was from your church, try not to be angry at the church and please don't be angry at God.

where was god?

Some children may wonder:

1) "Where was God when the abuse was happening to me?"

2) "Did I do something wrong?"

3) "Was I being punished by God?"

Do you believe God causes bad things to happen , like hurricanes, people dying and children being abused?

Harold Kushner is a *rabbi,* someone who studies and teaches his religion. He wrote the book *When Bad Things Happen To Good People.* Someone he loved died. Although he was very religious, he also wondered where God was and why God didn't save the person who died.

Rabbi Kushner finally decided that God doesn't *make* bad things happen. God helps us deal with life when bad things happen.

So instead of thinking that God may have caused the abuse, you may want to think about how God can help give you the strength to deal with what happened to you in the past.

the rainy day letter*

Sometimes children who were sexually abused get depressed. Depressed means feeling sort of sad, not having much energy, and feeling like there's no point in trying to do anything fun or interesting.

People who are depressed have a hard time remembering the good things that have happened to them in the past.

---

* "The Rainy Day Letter" is adapted from Yvonne Dolan's book *Resolving Sexual Abuse* (Norton, 1991) by permission of the author.

But when you feel pretty okay, you can write yourself a "Rainy Day" letter.

Write a list of your strengths and good memories of the past.

It's like a rainbow letter to look at on a day when the weather inside seems very gray and rainy.

It's a reminder that the sun comes out sometimes.

And you can feel good again.

Reading your list the next time you get sad just might help! What are some things you like to remember about yourself?

Draw a picture of yourself that shows best what you like about yourself.

What is the very best memory you have? What were the words, thoughts and feelings that went with that memory? Could you draw a picture of that memory?

what color is that feeling?

One reason why abuse is so painful is that your body remembers the uncomfortable feeling. Counseling helps get those feelings out of your body.

What were the colors of the uncomfortable feelings you had in the past? Color in the amount of uncomfortable feelings you are still experiencing.

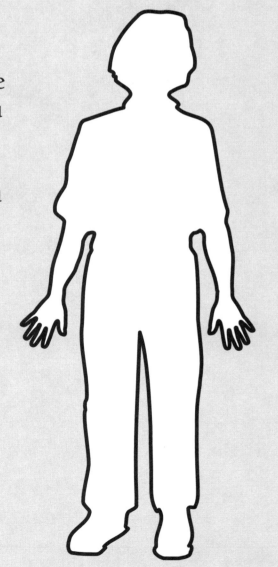

Remember one way to bring a good feeling back is to:

1) Think of the feeling.

2) Breathe the good feeling in.

And

3) Exhale the bad feeling out.

What positive feelings can
you color in your body instead?

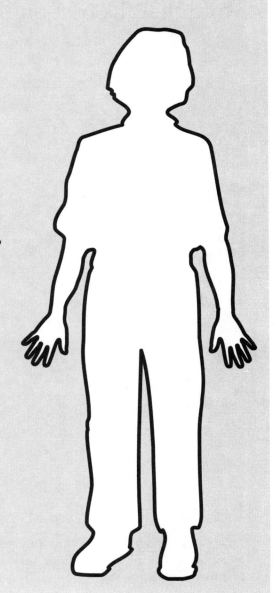

the I feel list*

Sometimes it's hard to know what you are feeling. For many children, when they are asked about their feelings, their answer is often, "I don't know." If that's like you, try using the "I Feel List" on the next page. Instead of saying "I don't know" you can choose the word that fits best on the next page.

---

* Title and Concept from *Treating the Young Male Victim of Sexual Assault: Issues & Intervention Strategies,* by Eugene Porter (1986), published by The Safer Society Press, Brandon, Vermont., by permission of the publisher.

"I feel" list

ANGRY - HAPPY	LOST - SECURE
HATEFUL - LOVING	WORTHLESS - WORTHY
DESPERATE - HOPEFUL	ANXIOUS - SERENE
LONELY - LOVED	ASSERTIVE - SHY
SHOCKED - CALM	STUPID - INTELLIGENT
SURPRISED - EXPECTANT	CLOSED-HEARTED
ISOLATED - SAFE	CURIOUS
SAD - JOYFUL	MEAN - KIND
DEPRESSED - LIGHT-HEARTED	TOUGH - TENDER
CONFUSED - CERTAIN	BELONGING - SEPARATION
AGGRESSIVE - LAZY	TIRED - ENERGETIC
COMPETITIVE - RETREATED	SARCASTIC - GENUINE
HYSTERICAL - PEACEFUL	ADEQUATE -INADEQUATE
CONFIDENT -SELF-CONSCIOUS	WARM - COLD
AFRAID - BRAVE	ALONE - CROWDED
LIKE - DISLIKED	ACCEPTED - REJECTED
CAREFUL - CARELESS	AROUSED - UNFEELING
INTERESTED -APATHETIC	SENSITIVE - DESENSITIZED
AWED - DISGUSTED	HARD - SOFT
RUSHED - AT EASE	PROTECTED - VULNERABLE
TENSE - RELAXED	CLEAN - DIRTY

anxious feelings are ok

When some children knew the abuse was about to happen they got anxious or nervous. They felt kind of upset and worried inside. Did that happen to you?

If that anxious feeling had a color what color would it be? What would be the color of the feeling while the abuse was going on?

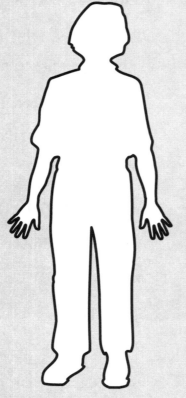

Anxious Feeling

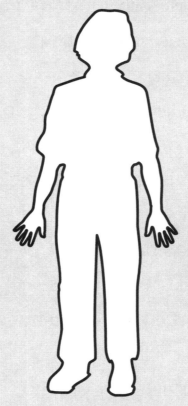

Abuse Feeling

Did you choose different colors for the anxious feeling and the abuse feeling because they are different?

Children get anxious about a lot of things ... and they learn to take that feeling away.

Counseling will help you deal with anxious feelings so they don't turn into abuse feelings. You don't need to be afraid of anxious feelings anymore. We all get them at times and we can make them go away.

other sad feelings

The sexual abuse you experienced may not be the only reason for your sad feelings.

Often times other things have happened to children that seemed just as BAD, or even worse than the abuse.

Some of the sad feelings came before the abuse, and others came after the abuse.

For some children the abuse only happened one time and for other children it happened many different times.

Color in the amount of sad feelings you had in each of the time periods below.

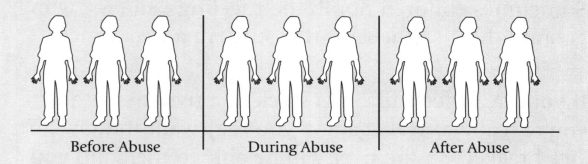

Before Abuse | During Abuse | After Abuse

Now that you have colored in your timeline, you and your therapist can talk about some of the other sad feelings in your life.

Does your timeline tell you that you have had more sad feelings before the abuse or after the abuse?

the ice breaker

Sometimes children numb their feelings, so they won't get hurt. It's like their heart is stuck in a river of ice.

If your heart feels like it is stuck in a river of ice, and you're ready to feel again ... you may want to draw an "ice breaker" so the river will be able to melt and you will be able to feel again.

The ice breaker can be an animal, a cartoon character, or something you have made up in your mind.

What does your ice breaker look like? Draw it here:

whose feeling is this?

Sometimes children who have been abused or neglected need to find out if the feelings they are having are really their own.

The next time you have a strong feeling about something ask yourself this question:

"Whose feeling is this?"

Have there been times in the past when it felt like someone else's feelings were in your body ... and your own feelings were LOST?

Write in your notebook or journal about one of those times. What were the feelings? Whose feelings might they be? What was happening? Draw a picture.

your family cartoon*

Sometimes children want to say things to a family member, but find that it's hard to get the words out. Other times, children wish those family members would say something to them.

Is there anything you want to say to a member of your family or that you would want them to say to you?

* Title and concept from Kee MacFarlane & Jill Waterman (1986), *Sexual Abuse of Young Children: Evaluation & Treatment*. New York: Guilford Press. Used by permission.

Feeling Good Again

Make your own family cartoon with the words you
want to say or you want to hear.

my timeline

It's always nice to look back so you can remember how far you have come . . . and to look forward to see how far you need to go. Color the figure that shows where you are now.

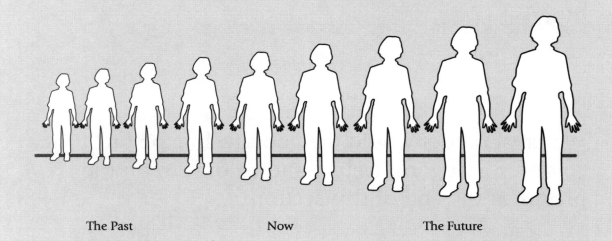

The Past   Now   The Future

understanding your feelings

Many children feel different about themselves at different times. Picture yourself with your good feeling on one shoulder and the uncomfortable feeling on the other.

Which shoulder would the good feeling be on? Pick a color for that good feeling and color it in on the picture at the end of this section.

Pick another color for the uncomfortable feeling and color that in.

Some feelings happen because of your self-talk, the pictures you make in your mind, and the words you remember other people saying.

Pick a time in your life where you need to have a better feeling. Fill in the picture to see how you need to change your self-talk, pictures, and words to remember.

understanding your feelings

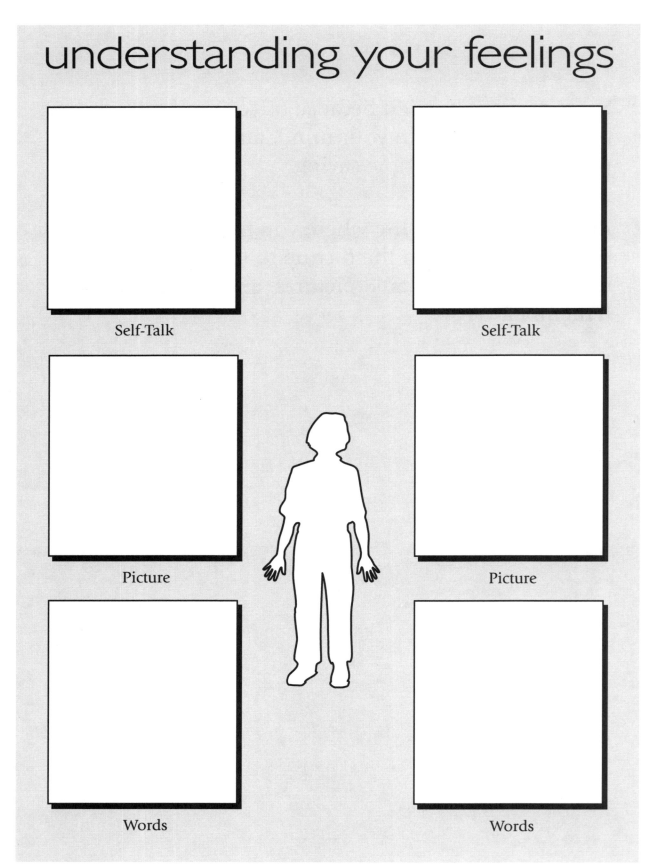

Self-Talk

Self-Talk

Picture

Picture

Words

Words

the angel from 1 minute before[*]

Suppose there was an angel on your shoulder 1 minute before the trauma you experienced. Although she couldn't stop what happened let's suppose that she was able to give you a message to help you get through the trauma. What would she say? Would you like to close your eyes so you can hear what she might have said?

Write down what you think the angel would say:

_____

_____

_____

_____

The next time you have a flashback or an uncomfortable thought about the trauma, you may want to remember what the angel said.

---

[*] Concept presented by Frank and "Eliezer" Gunzburg, Ph.D. (As adapted from the timeline work of Tad James) at the American Hypnosis Training Academy in Silver Spring, MD. It is included here by permission.

Part of the reason the abuse was so scary was because it was such a surprise. Some children are tricked, some are confused and some are afraid but most children are surprised at what was happening. Because they weren't prepared, they didn't know what to say or do.

Now that you are in counseling it's like you have your own angel from 1 minute before so you may not be surprised and you will have a better idea of what to do and say.

guardian angels

Do you believe in guardian angels? Some people think of guardian angels as their spiritual helpers.

Guardian angels remind us that we are not alone. If you had a guardian angel, what do you think he or she would look like?

Would they look like anyone you know? Would there be more than one angel?

Which shoulder would it be near?

Would you like to draw your guardian angel?

What are the messages the angel would tell you so you could feel safe? Write them here:

_____

_____

_____

_____

At what times in your life do you think you would need the angel to help you?

_____

_____

_____

_____

Another way to think about a guardian angel would be someone who would keep you company so that you are never alone.

What if your guardian angel was also sexually abused at one time? What do you think he or she might tell you to help you deal with what happened to you?

Guardian angels teach you to give to others. When you give your time, love and energy to help others, you often get back a lot more than you give.

The warm feeling that you get from being there and helping others is hard to describe but wonderful to have.

Sometimes when you step out of your own pain to help others, your own pain doesn't seem to hurt as much.

Is there anybody you have helped deal with their problems? Would you like to help someone in the future?

letter from the future

What will you be like in the future?

How will you be different?

How will you be wiser and stronger?

When the future comes, what do you want to be able to say to yourself about the past?

the storyteller

Trauma is when bad things happen, especially when it's very scary and there's nothing you can do to stop it.

Now that you are wiser and stronger than you were at the time of the trauma, you are ready to write a story to heal any part within you that is still suffering from the trauma.

What will your story be like?

Who will be the main character?

How will you recognize the child you were in the past?

On a separate piece of paper, write your story. Show it to your counselor.

your future self

Draw a picture of yourself doing something in the future. Think of this as a time when your trauma of the past is only a little part of all the memories you have.

brothers and sisters

If you have a brother or a sister, they would probably like to know what happened to you. If they haven't already been told, they may be wondering if the other family members are acting differently because they did something wrong.

Many families try to keep the abuse a secret from the other children. They think it will be too upsetting for them to know what happened.

Do you have a brother or sister who knows about what happened to you? If they don't know, you and your therapist may want to talk about this with your parents. If your brother or sister is older than you, they may be able to offer support. If you have a younger brother or sister, they may also have some questions.

If you have a brother or sister or other family member living with you, would you want them to know about what happened to you?

If you felt like there was a secret in your family that no one was telling you, would you worry about what was wrong? Lots of times our worries about things we don't know are worse than knowing.

If your brother or sister had been hurt in some way, would you want to know?

Sometimes when there are serious secrets in the family it is much harder for children to feel safe.

Part II

From Victim to Survivor

understanding your flashback

Children have flashbacks because they were frightened at the time of the abuse.

When children are frightened it is as if they go numb and freeze. Sometimes they even forget to breathe.

The thoughts, sounds, pictures and feelings from the abuse also get frozen in a tangled knot in their mind.

When children have flashbacks those same thoughts, sounds, pictures and feelings come back again because they are still in the same knot in their minds.

The purpose of counseling is to untangle the knot so you can learn what you need to know so the flashbacks will stop hurting.

The chart on the next page may help you understand your own flashback. Before you fill in the chart, make the picture of the abuse so small in your mind that it could fit into a TV that is small enough to fit in your watch.

Now you can get the information you need from the flashback, without bringing the uncomfortable feeling into your body.

a. Fill in the chart on the next page.

b. Outline each of the 4 boxes with a different color.

c. Trace each color over the line that represents each box to make the flashback knot on the next page.

d. Using the same colors, continue the lines and draw the way the flashback will look when it is untangled.

understanding your flashbacks

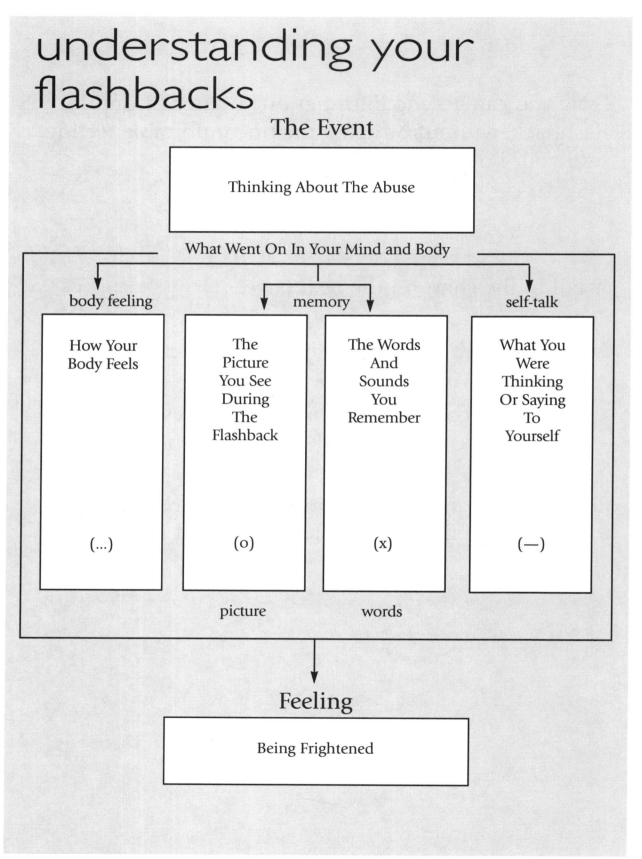

The Event

Thinking About The Abuse

What Went On In Your Mind and Body

body feeling

memory

self-talk

How Your Body Feels	The Picture You See During The Flashback	The Words And Sounds You Remember	What You Were Thinking Or Saying To Yourself
(...)	(o)	(x)	(—)

picture   words

Feeling

Being Frightened

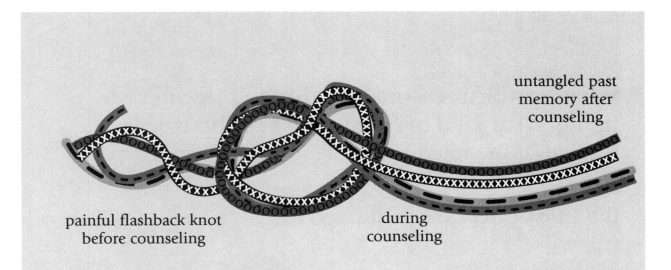

untangled past
memory after
counseling

painful flashback knot
before counseling

during
counseling

What could you think or say to yourself differently? Is there something your counselor has told you that you would remember?

What new picture would you like to place in your mind? What kind of feeling will your body have instead of the uncomfortable feelings from the past?

the title of my new picture is:

_____

_____

_____

The names of my new feelings are:

_____

_____

_____

Now that you understand how flashbacks are made ...

The next time you think of the abuse or start to have a flashback, you can change the way you react to the flashback so you will be able to stay calm.

changing how you react to the flashback

```
            ┌─────────────────────────────────────┐
            │       Thinking About The Abuse       │
            └─────────────────────────────────────┘
                             │
                             ▼
      ┌──────────────┬───────┴────────┬──────────────┐
      ▼              ▼                 ▼              ▼
  body feeling          memory                   self-talk
  ┌────────┐    ┌────────┐ ┌────────┐      ┌────────┐
  │        │    │        │ │        │      │        │
  │        │    │        │ │        │      │        │
  │        │    │        │ │        │      │        │
  └────────┘    └────────┘ └────────┘      └────────┘
                 picture      words
                        │
                        ▼
                    Feeling
            ┌─────────────────────────┐
            │      Staying Calm       │
            └─────────────────────────┘
```

Listed below are different qualities some children have found they need to control their flashbacks.

calmness   distance

energy   power

and   "being in the present"

Can you think of other ways to control your flashbacks?

needing to be energized

One girl another therapist was working with needed ENERGY to deal with her flashbacks. When she had a flashback all the energy went out of her. In order to get the feeling of energy that she needed, she did jumping jacks while she said the things she needed to say to get rid of the flashbacks, like:

"It wasn't my fault."

"I don't have to keep feeling the pain."

"This flashback happened in the past and I don't have to deal with it now."

The next time she started to have a flashback,she was able to bring the feeling of energy she had when she was doing the jumping jacks into her body.

That energy allowed her to picture different things, remember what her therapist said, and use her new self talk.

how safe? safety scales*

Scales are what people use to weigh or measure things. One kind of scale measures how much you weigh. Another kind of scale is more in a line, such as from 1 to 10. One end usually has a lot of what we're measuring, the other end not very much at all.

Using a "safety scale" we can measure how safe you feel at different times and places or with different people.

You probably feel safe with your therapist.

But how safe do you feel at other places that were dangerous in the past? On a scale of 1 (not at all safe) to 10 (totally safe), how safe do you feel at school? What number would you put on how safe you feel in your room at home?

It may be a good idea for you to talk with your therapist about how safe you feel at different places during the day.

_____

* "How Safe? Safety Scales" is adapted from Yvonne Dolan's book *Resolving Sexual Abuse* (Norton Publishing, 1991) by permission of the author.

If you don't feel safe now, what has to change so you will feel safe in the future?

If you are not living in your home but you plan to return to your home, your therapist and other helpers need to have a way to know that you are safe and doing okay, once you return home.

Can you think of how your therapist and other helpers will always know if you are safe?

the medicine bundle*

We all have things that give us pleasure and allow us to feel safe when we touch or look at them.

Those things could be a picture, a lucky stone, a special coin, your favorite charm or something you have made. These are the kinds of things that would be "good medicine" for you to help you feel better at times when you are feeling sad. What would you put into your "medicine bundle?"

---

* "The Medicine Bundle" is adapted from Yvonne Dolan's book *Resolving Sexual Abuse* (Norton Publishing, 1991) by permission of the author.

ranking your flashbacks

The more ways you look at your flashback, the better you will understand it. Another way to look at a flashback is to rank it. If 10 was the worst flashback you have ever had and 1 was the mildest … when you have a flashback you can ask yourself these 3 questions:

1. What number is the flashback I am having now?

2. What do I need to do to make it lower?

3. What else can I do to make it even lower?

robot or not

Philip Davidson, a therapist from Virginia, has a neat way of explaining flashbacks and other unwanted behaviors.

He draws a robot with a bunch of buttons.

Next he might ask the children he is working with some questions:

"Do you want to continue to allow your flashbacks (or someone else) to push your buttons and make you a robot?"

"Are you ready to stop allowing your flashbacks turn you into a robot?"

"Are there any people in your life who you *allow* to push your buttons?"

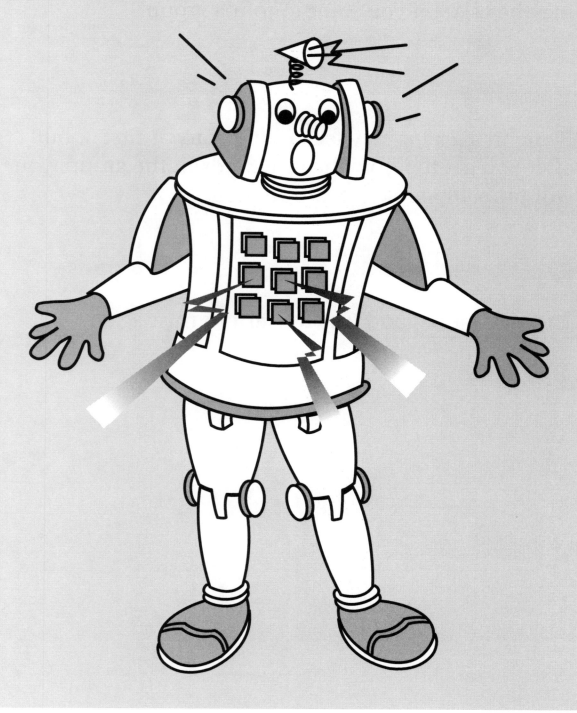

being in a group

After you work with your counselor one-to-one you may be asked if you want to join a group.

Being in a group may feel a little scary at first ... but after you get to know the other kids in the group, you will probably look forward to going to it.

The group is a good way to learn to trust again.

changing other behaviors

Some children develop behaviors that are not helpful and decide they would like to change them. Some examples of behaviors they may want to change might be that they are afraid to trust people; that they lose their temper easily; that they do poorly on tests when they get anxious; or even that they take things that don't belong to them from their homes and at school.

But guess what? It's not the event (being abused or having a flashback) that actually causes these behaviors. These behaviors come from how they think about events before the behavior. What that means is that when you want to change a behavior, the first thing you need to do is to change the thoughts and feelings you have before you decide to do the behavior.

Do you have any behaviors that you want to change?

The charts on the next pages may help you change a behavior you don't want anymore. Your first step is to gain a better understanding of the behavior, before you work on your solution behavior on the following page.

Ask your counselor to help you work on these charts.

understanding your behavior

Negative Behavior

The Event

feeling   memory   self-talk

picture   words

Feeling

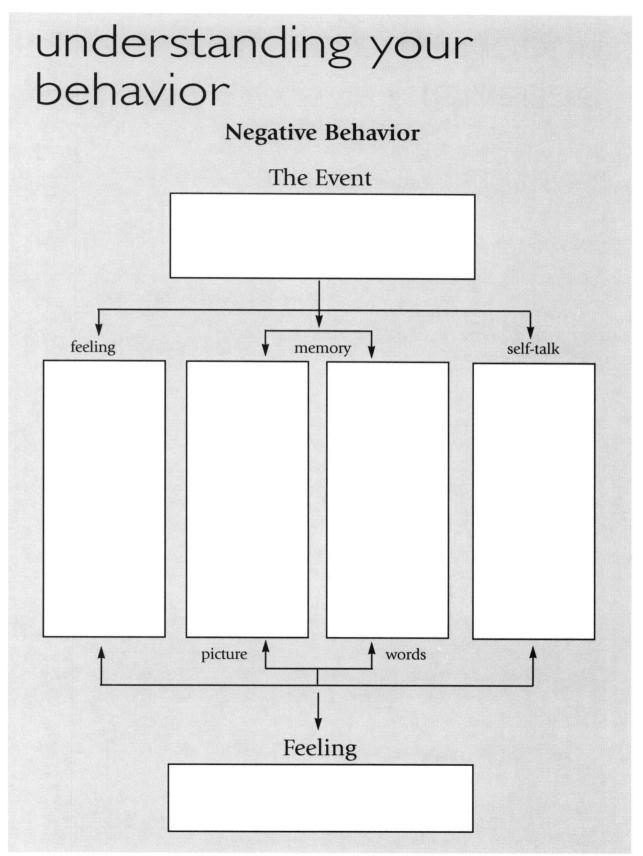

understanding your behavior

Solution Behavior

The Event

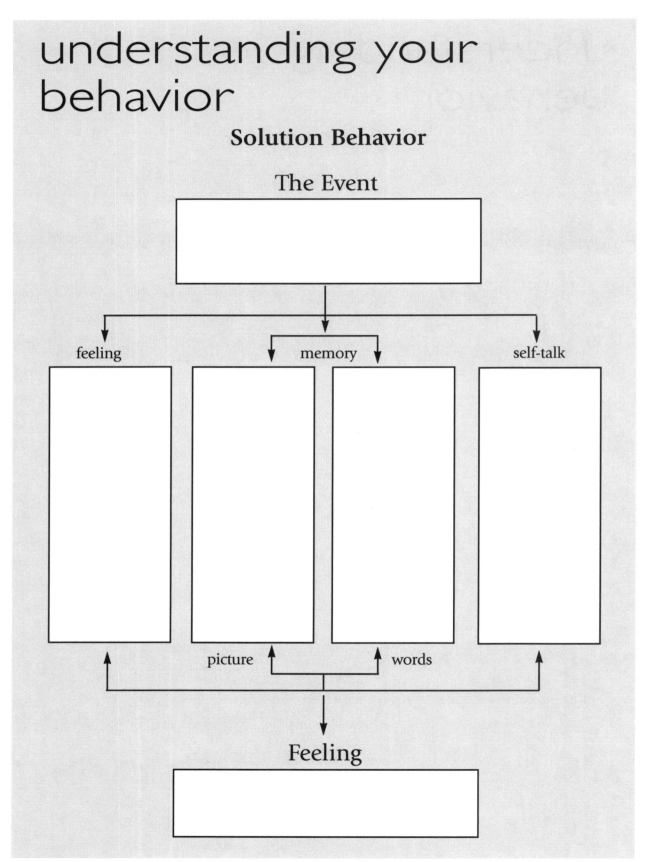

feeling   memory   self-talk

picture   words

Feeling

Part III

Feeling Good Again

your body is beautiful

You know what? Your body is amazing, incredible and beautiful. That's something to always remember.

Slow deep breathing is a good way to remind yourself of how wonderful your body is.

Deep breathing is also a good way to calm down and relax … especially after you think or talk about the abuse. It allows you to bring in pleasant and peaceful feelings, and breathe out all the uncomfortable feelings of the past.

Would you like to try some deep breathing and see how it works to relax you?

You may want to choose a color for your peaceful feeling and imagine that color filling your body until your body GLOWS with that peaceful feeling.

Take 5 long, slow deep breaths, and imagine that the air you breathe in will give you a peaceful feeling and the air you breathe out is the air that was making it hard for you to relax. The more you practice the better you will get in bringing the peaceful feeling into your body.

nothing is broken

Children who were abused sometimes feel like they are broken or "damaged" or spoiled for the rest of their lives. They may also feel dirty and ashamed. Those are feelings that belong to the abuser. If you sometimes feel that way, remember those feelings are not yours. You can picture yourself wrapping those feelings up in lots of newspaper and string and giving the whole mess back to the person who abused you, where they belong.

Some children who were abused in a violent physical way wonder if everything still works okay. Children who experienced pain as part of the abuse may think: "If it hurt, something must be broken."

Usually, everything in your body is okay or it will be okay after a while. The body is a wonderful thing because it knows how to heal itself so it is just like new. For most children, there is no permanent physical damage and no one will ever know they suffered abuse ... unless they want to tell someone.

getting clean enough

Some children don't feel like they can ever get clean enough. When they think about what happened to them they feel yucky and dirty.

But with their therapists they began to understand that they are not dirty and that what happened to them washed off a long time ago.

Since it is the *memory* of the abuse that makes them feel "dirty," thinking of a different memory may help them feel clean again.

One child imagined she saw all the dirt and fluids from the abuse run off her body and slide right down the drain.

Would you like to draw a picture of what that would look like for you? You can make your picture into a new memory, so when you think of the memory, it will help you feel clean again.

how am I feeling now?

As you have gone through your counseling sessions, you have learned to know how you are feeling NOW.

A good activity to do at the end of each counseling session is to remember and look at the feelings you had during that session.

Listed on the next page are some of the feelings you might have been experiencing. Before you look at the next page, make your own list so you can compare your list with the list on the next page.

1. _____

2. _____

3. _____

4. _____

5. _____

6. _____

Circle the feelings you have experienced during today's session:

confused	angry	sad
betrayed	numb	powerless
helpless	powerful	guilt
shame	embarrassed	proud
grateful	loved	accepted
understood	safe	fearful

List any other feelings you have also experienced below.

my parents are not me

When abuse occurs within the family, the child who was abused may feel very confused.

Children sometimes get angry at their parents.

A child may be angry at one parent for being abusive ... and angry at the other parent for not keeping the child safe.

These angry feelings may be very hard to deal with. It's hard to feel safe when you feel like your parent did something wrong or bad.

Children sometimes get the angry or "bad" feelings about their parents mixed up with their feelings about themselves. Some children think, "Well, if my parent was bad, maybe I'm bad." Others think, "My mother (or my father) couldn't be bad, so it must be me that's bad for thinking that."

That's a mistake in their thinking. If that is the way you're thinking, tell your counselor so he or she can help you figure it out.

It may help to think of the "bad" or "mad" feelings as feelings that come to visit, but they don't live inside you forever.

If you have angry feelings about your family, what color would these feelings be?

Remember, these angry colors don't live inside you. They visit sometimes, but they are other peoples' colors and are separate from you.

Draw a picture of your family and use the angry colors to color the person they belong to.

Having good feelings inside you about the people in your family that keep you safe can help you feel safe and comfortable.

If the good feelings had a color, what color would they be? Draw a picture of yourself with the good feelings color you get when you think about the good things about your family.

Remember! You don't have to let the angry feelings you have about the abuse or your family make you feel bad inside. You are not responsible for your whole family. You are only responsible for yourself and your feelings.

Everybody feels bad sometimes. Everybody feels angry sometimes, especially when their feelings are hurt. The colors of those feelings come to visit all children sometimes. But you can work on making sure they don't stay very long. We always want children to have all the good feeling colors of the rainbow in their bodies.

the old feelings rulebook

When children finish their therapy they often realize that they have learned different rules about dealing with feelings.

Can you remember what the old rules for feelings were like in your house? Write them down here.

Are there new and different rules for feelings in your house now? write them down here.

"my new thing"*

It's nice when you have a new thing in your life. New things allow you to concentrate on the present and make it easier not to think of old things.

Some new things of other children have been roller blading, ice-skating, karate, dancing, playing a new sport or reading a new bunch of books.

Do you have a new thing in your life that you can get totally involved in?

---

*"My New Thing" is adapted from Yvonne Dolan's book *Resolving Sexual Abuse* (Norton Publishing, 1991) with permission of the author.

turning problems into gifts

When you have a problem, after you get through it you are stronger, wiser, more sensitive, and better able to handle other problems in the future.

That is how you turn problems into gifts.

In your journal list some of the smaller problems you had in the past and ... how you turned them into gifts.

Dealing with sexual abuse may have been a big problem for you, not a little problem.

To turn it into a gift does not mean what happened to you was a good thing. It wasn't.

The gifts that came as a result of your getting through this Big problem are about what you learned, in what ways you got stronger, and how your life will change because of how you're dealing with what happened to you.

What were some of the ways that you became stronger, wiser and better able to take care of yourself?

1. _____

2. _____

3. _____

4. _____

5. _____

6. _____

putting the puzzle back together

There are always many pieces of a sexual abuse puzzle. The pieces are about:

1. Things that happened before the abuse started.

2. What was going on during the abuse.

3. What went on after the secret was out.

4. The new things you have learned in counseling and how you are feeling now.

One way to know when counseling is over is if you have talked about all the pieces of the abuse puzzle.

Look at the pieces of the abuse puzzle on the next page. Make a copy of the page.

Fill in the empty pieces with things that make it your own abuse puzzle. Now cut the pieces out and put the puzzle together.

And don't forget to save one piece for the last piece you fit into the puzzle.

It is the piece marked:

the end

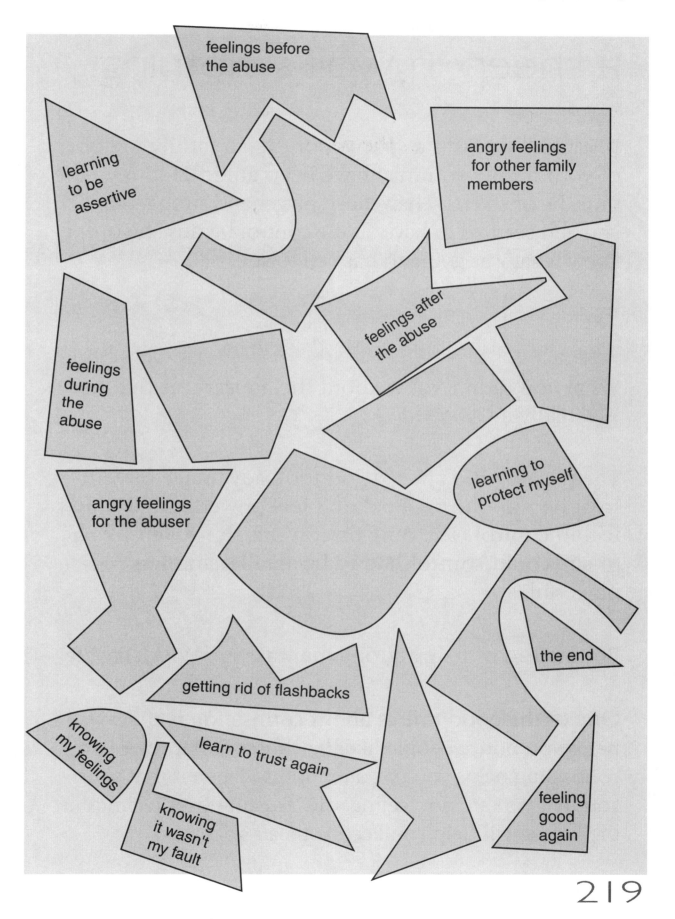

a sheep in wolf's clothing

If your abuser was a stranger or even a family member of your family you may have been afraid of him. At the time, he or she may have been bigger and stronger than you and seemed to have all the control because he or she knew what was going to happen to you.

What you didn't know about the abuser was that he was really a COWARD !

The person who abused you took advantage of your trust because he or she didn't feel powerful and didn't feel in control. The only person the abuser felt like he or she could control had to be smaller and less powerful.

But instead of being strong, he was very WEAK inside.

One of the good things about counseling is that it helps you notice people like the abuser. What you learn in counseling helps you pay attention to feelings that warn you that you are not feeling safe. Trusting your feelings in the future will help you keep yourself safer.

If you feel unsafe, you now know that you don't have to be fooled by the abuser.

And you know it's okay to scream and make people really be able to hear you.

You also know not to go places that don't feel safe, or to leave those places if you end up there anyway.

The picture you used to have in your memory of the abuser is probably very different than the one you have now.

Draw a picture of how you may want to remember the abuser now!

If the abuser still looks big and strong, have your counselor make some copies of the picture using the shrinking button on the copier so that each picture is smaller than the one before.

Now that you are bigger, smarter, faster, wiser, and quicker than you were when the abuse happened, draw a picture of yourself.

remembering

Children who were abused sometimes find it hard to remember what happened.

Not remembering is another way your mind protects you from looking at stuff you are not ready to deal with.

Later on you may remember more of what happened to you.

When that happens, it might feel a little scary. But it really just means you are getting

STRONGER !!!

How much of what happened can you remember now? Place an X on the parts of your body that were touched during the abuse.

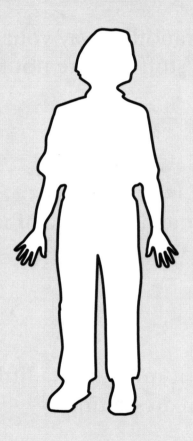

You can keep this drawing in a safe place to look at later if you forget or get confused.

love & sex

We all know that LOVE can be beautiful.

Sex can also be beautiful ... when it is combined with love and caring with a person who really cares for your well being.

Children who have been sexually abused get introduced to sex when it is about control and power instead of love.

When sex is combined with control and power it is not beautiful.

As you grow older, you will discover that sex can be beautiful with the right special person.

It will take time for you to trust again ... but once you do, and when the time is right, you will discover that sex can be beautiful.

Sex + Violence & Control = Abuse & Trauma

Sex + Loving & Caring = Safety & Pleasure

When children have been abused, all the words, thoughts and feelings that are related to sex may *seem* bad.

It will be important for your counselor to work with you on your thoughts and feelings about sex, love, growing up, and how your body will be changing in the future.

the pathway map

Joan Duhaime of Chesapeake, Virginia, asks children to draw a map so they can see where they are, how far they have progressed, and how far other family members may be on their journey of learning & growing. When they reach their own personal goals, they color in the blocks on their pathway map.

You and your therapist may want to make your own pathway map on a large poster board so you have enough room to write down all your goals & the pictures that go with them. Some questions that you may want to answer as you work on the map are listed below.

How did it feel when you first told about the abuse?

How have your feelings about yourself changed since you've been coming to counseling?

In what ways do you think you are healing and growing stronger?

Is there someone else in your family who also has to make some changes for the family to heal?

How do you think that person is doing?

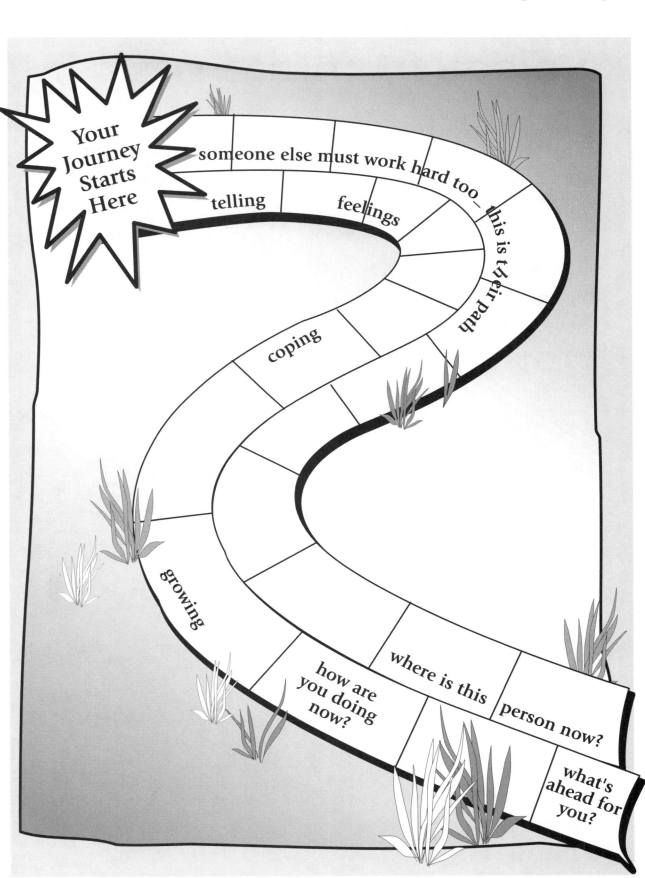

Your Journey Starts Here

someone else must work hard too — this is their path

telling

feelings

coping

growing

how are you doing now?

where is this

person now?

what's ahead for you?

a piece from the past

REMEMBER the abuse you survived is now just one piece from your past. It is not about who you are NOW !

There may have been some other unpleasant things in the past that you have already let go and forgotten. There may also have been some pleasant things that you want to remember.

Fill in the balloons on the next page with the memories and colors you want to hold on to and those you are ready to let go.

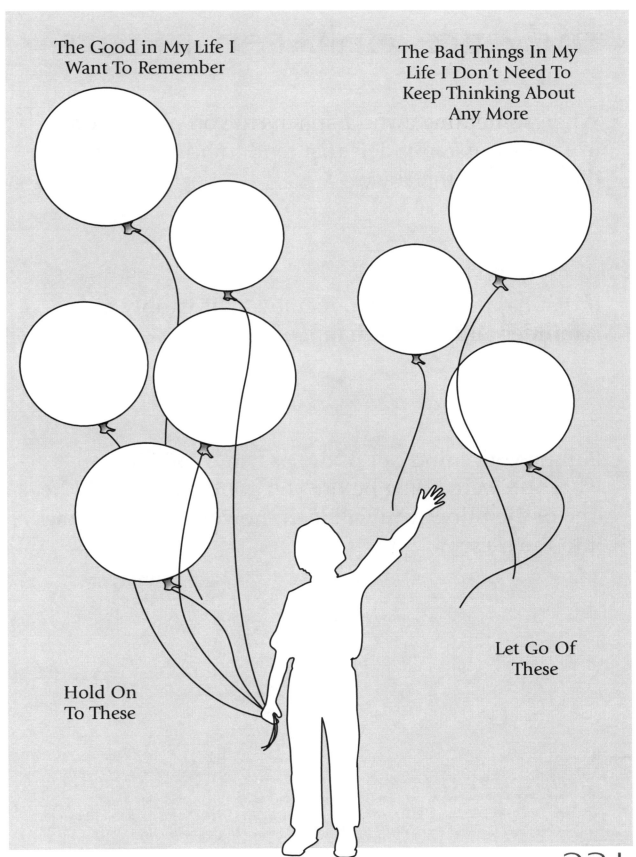

The Good in My Life I Want To Remember

The Bad Things In My Life I Don't Need To Keep Thinking About Any More

Hold On To These

Let Go Of These

231

they are only reminders[*]

When something awful happens to you, there are usually many reminders that tend to bring you back to the picture of the abuse.

If that happens to you, remember ... **it is only a reminder and it's not happening now.**

Pulling your mind out of the past and focusing on what you were doing before you got distracted will be one of the things you will learn how to do, to get back into the present.

---

*They Are Only Reminders was written (with permission) as a result of attending a workshop presented by Esther Deblinger, PHD. This concept is mentioned in her book, co-authored by Ann Heflin, *Cognitive Behavioral Therapy for Sexually Abused Children* (Sage Publishing, 1996).

memory vault

Some old memories can be painful. Most people would rather not remember painful old mmories. When you have these painful old memories, you might be spending a lot of energy keeping them from coming out. And then when you see your counselor and hear that you will need to talk about these old memories, you might be worried that the memories will come out all at once.

The memory vault is a good way to handle these memories.

A vault is a large steel safe. It is airtight, can be as big as a room, and it has a combination lock on its door.

Instead of using all that energy to keep the old memories hidden inside you, you can imagine letting those memories float out into the vault. Whenever you are ready to deal with one of those old memories, you can go to the vault and let one out.

You can let as much of the memory out that is ready to come out. The rest of the memory can stay locked up until you are ready to deal with it.

In this way, you can use your energy to have fun rather than to keep away old memories.

There are three things to remember about old memories.

1. It's okay if you can't remember them at all.

2. It's okay if you can just remember parts of a memory.

3. When a memory does begin to come back, it is a sign you are getting STRONGER !!

For some children old memories were scary because they never knew when they would come out. With the memory vault you can be in charge of when and where they come out. Most children bring the old memories out during their counseling session where they feel safe.

The important thing about the vault is that whenever you have a thought about the past that is troubling you, you can put it away until you feel it is safe to deal with. Are there other imaginary places like the memory vault that you could use to store old memories?

Carolyn Cunningham, who works with a lot of children who have been abused, suggested that you might want to draw your own memory vault and write in the memories you want to keep there.

After you do that you may want to decide which memories you are ready to work on and which ones you want to keep in the vault for a while.

Put a "1" next to the first memory you are ready to work on, "2" next to the second memory you think you want to work on, and then number as many memories as you can in the order you want them to come out.

If there are memories that you don't even want to think about for a while, you may want to draw a small safe inside the vault. In that way when you go in to let the other memories out one at a time, you don't even have to see the ones you put in the safe.

Draw your vault or the place you keep hard memories in the box below. Then draw or write the memories inside.

the concept puzzle

A concept is a piece of information to help you understand things better. It's an idea, or a way of looking at things. It might be a way of dealing with bad feelings. Jon Michael (who was 12 at the time)[*] completed this puzzle on the next page, about the concepts that he learned with his counselor. He didn't really like talking about what happened to him, but he was able to name some important concepts about abuse.

At the end of each session Jon and I named 3 or 4 concepts that had been discussed. Next, Jon wrote them in on the empty puzzle pieces.

---

[*]This name was made up by the person to protect the person's privacy.

Fill in the concepts on these puzzle pieces or make your own puzzle.

When all the puzzle pieces were filled up with concepts, Jon picked the five most important concepts and numbered them by how important they were.

The concepts that Jon and I figured out are listed on one of the next pages. Because everyone's experience is different, everyone's concepts are different.

After you make a list of the concepts that are related to your abuse, you may want to compare your concepts with Jon's.

List your concepts on this page.

Here is a list of some of Jon's concepts:

1. Run, Yell and Tell

2. I don't have to keep that crummy feeling in me anymore.

3. When children are abused, sometimes they think of all sex as a bad thing and it's not.

4. I have Nothing to be ashamed of.

5. I don't ever have to forgive the person who hurt me.

6. I am stronger than I thought I was.

7. If I want to forgive the person who hurt me, I can, when I am ready.

8. Sometimes people are mean to other people because someone was mean to them.

9. I am stronger, wiser, and can protect myself.

10. There is nothing wrong with me. There is something wrong with the person who hurt me.

11. Telling what happened to me may save someone else from getting hurt.

12. Most victims don't become abusers.

Were any of your concepts similar to Jon's?

Try ranking (putting a number on) your five most important concepts, and compare it to what Jon felt was most important for him.

1.

2.

3.

4.

5.

The five most important concepts for Jon were:

1. Abusers are cowards and bullies.

2. It was not my fault.

3. Time heals all wounds.

4. You don't have to give in to bullies even if they are bigger than you.

5. Stuffing feelings doesn't work.

new behaviors

Sometimes children are abused in ways that make them feel like there is no other choice. Abusers want children to think that way so that the abuse will continue.

Counseling helps you learn how you can make different choices and do different things in the future so you don't have to be afraid anymore.

What new behaviors did you learn?

When the abuse happens inside a family by one of the parents, the other parent may also try to feel numb, because he or she didn't want to believe something so awful was happening.

If you're in this situation, it will take time to forgive the parent who was numb and trust him or her to protect you.

This parent will need to learn how to protect you so you won't be abused again.

Listed on the next page are some behaviors other children have learned.

"I have found people that I can trust who care about me. They have told me I can call them anytime."

What does trust mean to you?

How do you know that it's okay to trust someone?

Who are the people you can trust? Write their names here.

Do you have their phone numbers? Write them down here.

"I know where I can go if I need to get to a safe place."

Do you have a safe place to go?

In your neighborhood, are there any safe places that have a "safe place" sign like the one below? Do you know where they are?

"When I don't feel right about something or I have questions I need to have answered, I talk to someone about it."

"When I am not sure how someone is feeling, I ask them. I try not to guess at what they are feeling, because I may be wrong.

"I have learned that I am important. If I feel someone is not being honest with me or that they should have protected me, I will tell them."

"When I am with younger family members, I show them how to protect themselves and be safe."

"If I see children in the neighborhood touching other younger children, I tell someone so those children can get help too."

"If anyone touches me, I know I can yell and tell them to STOP! and I know I can tell someone ... even if it seemed like an 'okay' touch."

"I know that most adults who abuse children usually know those children.

They are nice at first and start off with good touches."

"I tell all adults who I don't know very well that I don't like to be touched at all."

"Sometimes even family members sexually abuse their children. I know now if I am uncomfortable with the way any family member is touching me, talking to me or even looking at me, I will talk to that family member and someone else about the way that person makes me feel. I also know that the sexual relationships my parents have with each other should be separate from their relationship with me."

intersecting hearts

Sometimes when children are abused they forget that there is still a lot of love in the world. Peter Michel, an artist and sculptor, shows that concept with a work he called "Intersecting Hearts."*

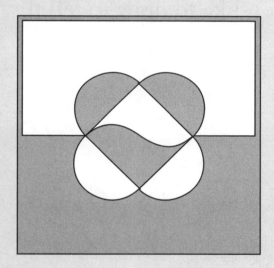

Are there other ways that you could draw hearts that intersect? When you draw hearts is it easier to feel all the love in the world?

Is there something else you can draw that shows love in the world?

---

*Used by permission of Peter Michel Clinton, NY (315) 853-8146.

you are not alone

Artist Peter Michel created the design* below. It was his way of conveying the concept that you are not alone.

He calls this work "Support Circle."

What would you like to draw to tell the world that you are not alone?

*Used by permission of Peter Michel of Clinton, NY (315) 853-8146.

Although it may sometimes seem that you are alone, there will always be someone there for you, as long as you look for them.

There will always be someone in front of you who you could reach to for support and someone behind you that you may want to reach back to help along their journey of healing.

*Used by permission of Peter Michel Clinton, NY (315) 853-8146.

hope scale*

It's OK to hope.

Hope is when you believe deep inside you that things will get better.

Many children have lived in families where the abuse had taken place for so long ... they forgot how to hope.

Other children have lived with a parent whose problems with alcohol and drugs became more important than their love for their children.

Those children also experienced many broken promises.

For some of them hoping for change may have felt terrifying because it was just another way to be disappointed again.

*Hope Scale was written (with permission) as a result of attending a workshop presented by Esther Deblinger, PHD. This concept is mentioned in her book, co-authored by Ann Heflin, *Cognitive Behavioral Therapy for Sexually Abused Children* (Sage Publishing, 1996).

If the number 10 represented the most hope you could have:

What number would you give yourself at the time the abuse was going on?

Place that number here.

What number would you give yourself now?

Place that number here.

What number on the hope scale would you like to have when you are ready to stop counseling?

Place that number here.

I hope your hope scale number has changed.

For many children, their hope scale changed once they told someone about the abuse.

If your hope scale hasn't changed very much, the best thing you can do is to keep talking to your counselor about your feelings.

If you still have worries and fears, your counselor needs to know. You need to talk about them. And then maybe your hope scale numbers will begin to change.

Part IV

More Questions

what happened to my family?

Sometimes, sexual abuse happens in a family. One of the family members, a parent, a brother or sister, or another relative is the abuser. When that happens, members of the family are often separated.

Sometimes, when that happens, the child who told about the abuse may feel like it's his or her fault that the family has been split up.

If you are feeling responsible, remember that you were not the one in your family who did the wrong thing. The person who abused you did the wrong thing, not you.

It was not your fault. You are not responsible for what happened.

You did the right thing when you told somebody.

The person in your family who abused you was at fault. That person caused the mess.

If you have a brother or sister who is angry at you, that person needs to know that what you did may have prevented the same thing from happening to them.

why is there so much anger in my family?

Did you ever play hot potato?

No one can hold the "hot potato" so they keep passing it along to someone else so they don't get burned. Anger in the family is like holding a hot potato. No one wants to hold it too long. So they pass it on to someone else in the family.

When the abuse happened inside a family, sometimes the anger about the abuse comes out in different ways. It's like a hot potato ... because it jumps all around from one person to the other.

was it just a mistake?

Sometimes when the abuse happens in the family it often seems innocent ... as if it were a mistake.

Mistakes do happen in families, because sometimes parents also get confused ... or they just don't realize that they have done something wrong. If the touching happened more than one time, chances are, what happened wasn't a mistake.

The important thing is that you told someone, and you have better ways to protect yourself in the future.

everybody knows

Sometimes it seems like everybody knows about what happened to you. You may live in a small town or you may have a friend who has a BIG MOUTH!

Even if people are talking about what happened to you ... remember that they will probably get tired of their gossip very soon, and eventually it will drift out of their minds.

And maybe because they did talk about it, it might have helped someone else to speak out about their own abuse, or warned other children to be careful about their bodies around a particular adult.

should I tell my friend?

Is this a question you have already asked? If you think telling a friend might help you feel better, it may be something you want to do. If the abuse happened within your family, you may want to talk to another family member, before you tell a friend.

Remember to be very careful about who you choose to share your feelings with. How will you decide who you can tell? What have you learned about deciding who you can trust? Sometimes friends may not really understand what happened to you.

Sometimes friends feel confused. They might have a lot of the same questions you had. Some might even want to talk about it to other people, or even gossip about it. Be sure your friend is understanding, someone you can really trust to keep your private things private.

If you would not tell your friend about other private things then you might not want to tell this friend about the abuse.

The abuser's behavior is not private because it hurts others, but your experience and your body are yours and can be private.

why did he expose himself?

"Mary" came to see me to talk about being sexually abused.

Mary's brother was also sexually abused. One day he did a strange thing ... He showed his private parts to Mary!

Mary was shocked and embarrassed.

She was also very confused. Why did he do that?

Sometimes we don't know all the answers. What we do know, is that sometimes when children are abused, they ACT OUT in different ways.

Sometimes they touch themselves too much or at the wrong times, other times they might expose themselves, or try to be friendly to others in a sexual way. Their "acting out" behavior doesn't seem to be something they really want to do.

It is more like some part of them, that they still don't understand, needs to "act out." It is like that part is saying:

"It still hurts and I need to get that yucky feeling out."

Sexually acting out on themselves or on others will not really help children who have been abused feel better. Sexual acting out is a SIGNAL that a child needs to talk to someone to try to get the hurt and confusion out.

It may be really hard for others to talk about sexual behaviors they have done. They may even deny they did it. Try to be patient and supportive to other family members so they can get help and not feel any worse about themselves. sometimes being supportive means telling someone who can help, so the secret can come out.

if he loved me why did he do it?

The person who abused you needs to learn a different way to show you that he (or she) loves you. That's why this person is in counseling.

It might be that when this person was young, he (or she) may also have been abused. One of your goals in counseling will also be to learn healthy ways to show others you love them.

Remember, there are many ways to show how much you care about someone. Can you think of ways to show you care about someone? Children who were abused sometimes think touching someone is the only way to show they care.

why did he do it?
why did she do it?

Listed below are some reasons another child might have molested you.

He or she might have been trying to control you, hurt you, or shock you.

He or she may not have been thinking clearly.

He or she might have wanted to see what it felt like to do something that was "bad."

He or she might be selfish and not thinking about how you would feel.

He or she might have felt weak and molested you to feel strong.

Can you think of any other reasons?

does this make me gay?

Boys who were sexually abused by older boys or men often have questions about what their abuse really means. Girls abused by other girls or by adult women may have the same questions.

Does it mean they are gay because they were sexually touched by a person of the same sex? The answer is NO!

Most abusers are not gay. Adults who are sexually attracted to children are called pedophiles. Most pedophiles are not gay (that is, they are not interested in being sexual with adults of the same sex).

can I make him gay?

Sometimes when a boy has been sexually abused by a boy or a man, he thinks he did something to make another male attracted to him.

He feels that somehow it was his fault and that there must be something wrong with him.

Boys who feel this way sometimes stay away from their own brothers, uncles and even their fathers. They are afraid they will make them gay. That is a big mistake that comes from confused thinking.

These boys are not gay because they have been molested by a male, and they cannot make anyone else gay.

what if somebody I know is gay?

Some boys are afraid of men who are gay. They are afraid these men may make sexual advances toward them. The boys are even afraid that "gayness" will rub off on them as if it were something they could catch, like the measles or the flu.

Most gay men are like most other men; they are not attracted to children. They like to be with other men.

Gay women (lesbians) are attracted to other adult women, not to children.

Being gay is not something you can catch. It is not the same as being abusive. Most gay people are not abusive, just like most other people are not abusive. If your teacher or anyone else you know is gay, you will probably learn that there is not much difference between him or her and other people you know.

Some experts think that gay people are born with an attraction to people of their own sex and age. But many gay men and lesbians (gay women) say they weren't sure they were gay until they were older teenagers or young adults.

Children and young teens often try out sexual things with each other, like kissing. As long as both people agree and give their consent and there is no sense of one person having more power, it is okay and normal. Most children do same sex behaviors with children their own age before age 12. And most of those children do not grow up to be gay.

did this happen to other boys?

About half of the children who have been sexually abused are boys. You are not alone.

Some boys and their families don't talk about the abuse because they feel ashamed, even though they they do not deserve it. Some families start off thinking it might have been the boys' fault ... or that their son should have fought harder. This is a mistake in their thinking.

Because some people keep the abuse of boys a secret, the boys who are abused have no idea how many other boys have had experiences just like theirs.

did this happen to other girls?

At least half of the children who have been sexually abused are girls. You are not alone.

Some girls and their families don't talk about the abuse because they feel ashamed, even though they do not deserve it. Some families start off thinking it might have been the girl's fault ... or that their daughter should have fought to get away or shouldn't have worn a pretty dress. This is a mistake in their thinking.

Because some people keep it secret when a girl in their family has been sexually abused, it's hard for a girl to know that what has happened to her has happened to a lot of other girls, too.

Feeling Good Again

Sometimes children have engaged in sexual play with other children before they were abused. They wonder if that maybe made them gay. Those children may have even wondered if the abuser somehow knew about it and picked them to abuse because of that.

But, guess what?! All children are sexual and have sexual feelings. Many children do sexual things with their childhood friends. Most of those things are very normal.

If you have worries or questions about your own sexual feelings or behavior that have nothing to do with the abuse, be sure to ask your counselor about those things too.

can I still care for the person who abused me?

The abuser may be someone you still care about a lot, like a parent, an uncle or aunt, or a cousin, or even someone outside the family who was nice to you except for the abuse. After what happened to you, that may be confusing for you.

The person who abused you may have some good qualities. Abusers are not always bad people. Instead, it is their behavior that is bad and abusive.

After the abuser gets counseling and apologizes for what he or she did to you, you may want to allow this person back into your life in a different way than before. Or you may not.

The most important thing is for you to be safe. If you and your therapist can figure out ways for you to be safe around this person, maybe it would work. But it is sometimes hard for older abusers to see exactly when they start feeling and acting sexual around you or treating you differently.

what if I hurt someone else?

Sometimes, children who have been sexually abused try to keep it secret, along with all their feelings. But then the uncomfortable feelings that they are trying to keep inside come out on others.

When they abuse other children with sexual touching it allows them to feel like the one in control instead of feeling like the victim. Being angry all the time, getting into fights, and acting like a bully is like that, too.

Part of your counseling will be to help you to deal with any of your hurtful behaviors so that it doesn't happen again. Then you can apologize to the child you hurt, and you can forgive yourself for what you did.

somethings to remember

Trauma is like cement.

If you wait too long to talk about it, it starts to harden. It's better to talk about it now than to wait.

Uncomfortable feelings are SIGNALS that you need to make a change.

Dealing with emotional pain in your past will help you to manage other pain in the future.

And most important of all, remember that ...

what happened to you doesn't make you any less SPECIAL!

saying goodbye

Is there anything you want to say to the therapist who has been working with you?

Can you list three things that you have learned about yourself and the abuse?

1.

2.

3.

summary

A lot has probably happened since you first told about your abuse. Many feelings, some pleasant and some not so pleasant, probably came out.

You may have also begun to feel stronger, wiser and safer. As you grow older, some thoughts about the abuse may come back. If that happens to you, you may want to talk to someone, like a counselor or therapist, about those thoughts.

The most important thing is that the secret has come out and you can now be in control of your life.

bibliography

Calderon, M.S. & Ramey, J.W. (1982). *Talking with Your Child About Sex.* New York: Random House.

Capacchione, L. (1988). *The Power of Your Other Hand.* North Hollywood, CA: Newcastle Publishing Co. Inc.

Cunningham, C. & MacFarlane, K. (1996) *When Children Abuse.* Brandon, VT: The Safer Society Press.

Dolan, Y. (1991). *Resolving Sexual Abuse.* New York: Norton.

Friedrich, W. (1990). *Psychotherapy of Sexually Abused Children and Their Families.* New York: Norton.

Hagans, K.B. & Case, J. (1988). *When Your Child Has Been Molested.* New York: Lexington.

Haugaard, J. & Repacci, N.D. (1988). *The Sexual Abuse of Children.* San Francisco: Jossey-Bass.

Hindman, J. (1983). *A Very Touching Book.* Ontario, OR: Alexandria Associates.

Loiselle, M.B. & Wright, L.B. (1997). *Shining Through: Pulling It Together After Sexual Abuse.* Brandon, VT: The Safer Society Press.

MacFarlane, K. & Waterman, J. (1986). *Sexual Abuse of Young Children: Evaluation & Treatment.* New York: Guilford.

Mather, C.L. with Debye, K. (1994). *How Long Does it Hurt?* San Francisco: Jossey-Bass.

Porter, E. (1986). *Treating the Young Male Victim of Sexual Assault: Issues & Intervention Strategies,* Brandon, VT: The Safer Society Press.

Sgroi, S.M. (1982). *Handbook of Clinical Intervention in Child Sexual Abuse.* Lexington, MA: Lexington Books.

Wolinsky, S. (1993). *The Dark Side of the Inner Child.* Norfolk, CT: Bramble Co.

Wasserman, B. (1994). *Stories for Children with Problems and Wishes: A Therapeutic Workbook for Turning Problems into Gifts.* Minneapolis, MN: Educational Media.

Select Safer Society Publications

Back on Track: Boys Dealing with Sexual Abuse by Leslie Bailey Wright and Mindy Loiselle (1997). A workbook for boys ages 10 and up. Foreword by David Calof. $14.

Shining Through: Pulling It Together After Sexual Abuse SECOND EDITION by Leslie Bailey Wright and Mindy Loiselle (1997). A workbook for girls ages 10 and up. $14.

STOP! Just for Kids: For Kids with Sexual Touching Problems Adapted by Terri Allred and Gerald Burns from original writings of children in a treatment program (1997) $15.

When Children Abuse: Group Treatment Strategies for Children with Impulse Control Problems by Carolyn Cunningham and Kee MacFarlane. (1996). $28.

Tell It Like It Is: A Resource for Youth in Treatment by Alice Tallmadge with Galyn Forster (1998). Interviews with teens in treatment for sexually abusive behavior. $15.

The Relapse Prevention Workbook for Youth in Treatment by Charlene Steen (1993). $15.

Pathways: A Guided Workbook for Youth Beginning Treatment by Timothy J. Kahn (Revised Edition 1997). $15.

Pathways Guide for Parents of Youth Beginning Treatment by Timothy J. Kahn (Revised Edition 1997). $8.

Mother-Son Incest: The Unthinkable Broken Taboo — An Overview of Findings by Hani Miletski (1995). $10.

Man-to-Man, When Your Partner Says NO: Pressured Sex & Date Rape by Scott A. Johnson (1992). $6.50.

From Trauma to Understanding: A Guide for Parents of Children with Sexual Behavior Problems by William D. Pithers, Alison S. Gray, Carolyn Cunningham, & Sandy Lane (1993). $5.

Adolescent Sexual Offender Assessment Packet by Alison Stickrod Gray & Randy Wallace (1992). $8.

Sexual Abuse in America: Epidemic of the 21st Century by Robert E. Freeman-Longo & Geral T. Blanchard (1998). $20.

Personal Sentence Completion Inventory by L.C. Miccio-Fonseca, PhD (1998). $50, includes ten inventories and user's guide. Additional inventories available in packs of 25 for $25.

When You Don't Know Who to Call: A Consumer's Guide to Selecting Mental Health Care by Nancy Schaufele & Donna Kennedy (1998). $15.

Assessing Sexual Abuse: A Resource Guide for Practitioners edited by Robert Prentky and Stacey Bird Edmunds (1997). $20.

Impact: Working with Sexual Abusers edited by Stacey Bird Edmunds (1997). $15.

The Difficult Connection: The Therapeutic Relationship in Sex Offender Treatment by Geral T. Blanchard (1998). $12.

Supervision of the Sex Offender by Georgia Cumming and Maureen Buell (1997). $25.

A Primer on the Complexities of Traumatic Memories of Childhood Sexual Abuse: A Psychobiological Approach by Fay Honey Knopp & Anna Rose Benson (1997) $25.

The Last Secret: Daughters Sexually Abused by Mothers by Bobbie Rosencrans (1997). $20.

Men & Anger: Understanding and Managing Your Anger for a Much Better Life by Murray Cullen & Rob Freeman-Longo. Revised and updated, new self-esteem chapter. (1996). $15.

When Your Wife Says No: Forced Sex in Marriage by Fay Honey Knopp (1994). $7.

Female Adolescent Sexual Abusers: An Exploratory Study of Mother-Daughter Dynamics with Implications for Treatment by Marcia T. Turner & Tracey N. Turner (1994). $18.

Adult Sexual Offender Assessment Packet prepared by Mark Carich & Donya Adkerson (1995). $8.

Who Am I & Why Am I in Treatment? A Guided Workbook for Clients in Evaluation and Beginning Treatment by Robert Freeman-Longo & Laren Bays (1988; 8th printing 1997) First workbook in a series of four for adult sex offenders. Also available in Spanish. $12.

Why Did I Do It Again? Understanding My Cycle of Problem Behaviors by Laren Bays & Robert Freeman-Longo (1989; 6th printing 1997). Second in the series. $12.

How Can I Stop? Breaking My Deviant Cycle by Laren Bays, Robert Freeman-Longo, & Diane Montgomery-Logan (1990; 5th printing 1997). Third in the series. $12.

Empathy and Compassionate Action: Issues & Exercises: A Workbook for Clients in Treatment by Robert Freeman-Longo, Laren Bays, & Euan Bear (1996). Fourth workbook in a series of four for adult sex offenders. $12.

The Safer Society Press is part of The Safer Society Foundation, Inc., a 501(c)3 nonprofit national agency dedicated to the prevention and treatment of sexual abuse. To receive a catalog of our complete listings, please check the box on the order form (next page) and mail it to the address listed or call us at (802) 247- 3132. For more information on the Safer Society Foundation, Inc., visit our website at http://www.safersociety.org.

Order Form

Date: _____

All books shipped via United Parcel Service. Please include a street location for shipping as we cannot ship to a Post Office box address.

Shipping Address:

Name and/or Agency _____

Street Address (no PO boxes) _____

_____

City _____ State _____ Zip _____

Billing Address (if different from shipping address):

Address _____

_____

City _____ State _____ Zip _____

Daytime phone (_____) _____

P.O. # _____

Visa or MasterCard # _____

Exp. Date _____

Signature (FOR CREDIT CARD ORDER)_____

☐ Please send a catalog.   ☐ Do not add me to your mailing list.

QTY	TITLE	UNIT PRICE	TOTAL COST

All orders must be prepaid.
Make checks payable to:

Sub Total		
VT residents (only) add sales tax		
Shipping (see below)		
TOTAL		

SaferSocietyPress
PO BOX 340
BRANDON, VT 05733-0340

All prices subject to change
without notice. No Returns.
Bulk discounts available, please inquire.
Call for quote on rush orders.

Shipping & Handling
1-5 items - $5   6-10 items - $10
11-15 items - $15   15-20 items - $20
21-25 items - $25   26-30 items- - $30
31+ items - $35

Phone orders accepted with
MasterCard or Visa. Call (802) 247-3132.